THE
WESTONBIRT
WISHES

Published as part of the
Westonbirt International Festival of the Garden
John Newling "Westonbirt Wishes"
Westonbirt, The National Arboretum

Published by SWPA Limited
publishing@swpa.com

ISBN 0 9547300 1 1
Copyright 2004 © John Newling and Sam Wilkinson

Curated by Sam Wilkinson
Edited by Anne Newling and Alan Ward, Axis
Photographs: John Newling, Paul Hough and Andy Love
Publication Design: www.axisgraphicdesign.co.uk

THE
WESTONBIRT
WISHES

JOHN
NEWLING

SWPA

The Westonbirt Wishes

The artist John Newling is noted for his ability to construct works that are both informed by the context of a place and that inform in return. His work frequently uses data. The work 'Cartography of Desire' generated lottery numbers; 'Weight' forensically cleaned 50,000 two pence coins to discover the fiscal value of dirt; 'Skeleton' and 'Stamping Uncertainty' employ a hymnal's worth of the questions held in hymns.

John Newling's projects involve transactions. His work includes the situation formed between people and his works. This can be seen from his commissioning of a street vendor of commercial art as part of an installation in Dublin to the public being invited to operate his projection machines outside the wall of Stafford prison and the more recent silent bidding in relation to a series of charity shop projects,

As a precursor to a commission to install a work at the Westonbirt National Arboretum Newling wrote the following short essay:

Imagine if spring didn't come ...

Imagine if spring didn't come. This weekend has been filled with spring sunshine. Blossom has appeared on trees, early flowers are growing, and spring is on its way. People, conscious of a confirmation of the season or not, are lightened and more positive. There is a sense of relief that what we had hoped for is happening, a kind of confirmation of faith.

From our earliest origins we have been conscious of fundamental clocks from our environment. Night and day, sun and moon, spring, summer and winter are embedded in our human psyches. Our earliest fears were largely formed against a common anxiousness that the annual patterns might not continue.

If spring did not follow winter or day did not follow night survival, the passing on of genes, would be challenged. Such patterns of nature became a crucial measure of our existence. It was a matter of belief that day would follow night. Beliefs are subject to change and our earliest beliefs generated numerous strategies to support our wish, our desire for the patterns in nature to be maintained.

The anxiety of questioning whether or not the sun will rise is replaced by a trust that it will. Such a trust in nature's pattern is faith. Many pagan rites are largely our attempt to generate faith in nature's pattern. Faith as an absolute trust frees us from constant questioning and anxiety and allows us to pursue other aspects of survival that can evolve towards a community. The possibility that the rhythms of the natural world could be fractured is equated with our only certainty; our death.

With the progress made in recent years in understanding genetics and brain biology there has been a suggestion of a

neural network that may function as a centre of belief. Given the relationship of our view of nature in terms of our mortality it is possible that our early neural evolution had at its centre a system that looked to acknowledge our death whilst advocating beliefs that seek to counter the finality of death.

Such a seeking may be uniquely human. To seek to contextualise death as part of a greater cycle is a necessary part of evolving a belief in the non-empiric as a constituent of a desire for faith.

As a review of mortality this is an evolution that decentres the dominant pattern of nature and our death and places us in a position of freedom from such a pattern. It positions us in a mind set that can move away from the fear that will spring not come and towards a belief in our continuity. It acknowledges the power of nature whilst needing to posit many thoughts that would allow us to transcend nature as our death.

The making of wishes and the posing of questions are the flux of humanity; questioning drives us forward and the consequent revolutions in thought allow us to evolve. It is the nature of some questions that they are unanswerable, and this is where the unprovable becomes a fuel of being human. We could wish for a difference

Thus, wishing and questioning are very human activities that have allowed us to survive against the vicissitudes of nature. However, it becomes necessary to stop questioning and wishing that things will happen. We need to have faith; we need to trust.

This work will take the form firstly of questions, of wishes. People will be invited to scribe their wish or question onto a ribbon. The ribbons will then be attached to a specific part of a specific tree. The ribbons will not be spaced over the tree like Christmas decorations. Rather they will be attached to one spot so that, ribbon by ribbon, they grow into a bolus. This lumpen form becomes a cipher for our humanity in relation to the structure of the tree. It is a sculpture within a sculpture.

In the early summer of 2003 John Newling installed his work 'If Spring Never comes ...'

Building upon previous projects using wishes and questions Newling hoped to establish for Westonbirt a situation where wishes, in the form of data, would evolve to create a form; a form that could eventually be cast in bronze. Newling's interest here is in the fact that a bronze cast would be a hollow form whose interior void had been occupied by many thousands of desires. It would have a surface whose skin, formed from such a traditional material that is so unlike the human qualities that make up its interior form.

The sculpture had initially been titled 'Collecting Questions & Wishes'. The installation acted as a bureau where people visiting the arboretum were invited to write their wishes or questions onto ribbons. The ribbons, along with their wishes, were then transferred to an adjacent oak tree. Ribbon by ribbon, they did indeed grow into a bolus. For the duration of the installation the project became a union between the beauty of the trees and the human desires that were reflected in the needs and uncertainties expressed in the wishes and questions.

The bureau took the form of a steel table alongside a stainless steel collection cabinet. These objects sat a short distance away from the tree that had been selected within the project site. The magnificence of the tree was countered by the simple industrial forms of the bureau. A space was chosen on the tree's branch where the volume of wishes would grow as people entered into the transaction of the project.

Several miles of ribbon were purchased and cut into the requisite lengths, pens were provided and the team on site, led by Phil Morton were briefed to undertake the twin tasks of recording the wishes and applying them, wish upon wish, to the branch. In this manner a for emerged upon the skin of the tree.

Such was the response to the installation that within a few weeks it became evident that more ribbon would be required. It was apparent that people were responding with care and consideration. The wishes being recorded were funny, odd and extremely moving. The project demonstrated a clear need for petition; it allowed people to express loss and hope, fear and desires.

Over the following weeks more and more ribbon was tracked down, bought and cut. The Arboretum Ranger team worked tirelessly to ensure that the project was properly maintained. The data being collected was a fascinating snap shot of people's desires and questions in this early year of a new millennium. What was eventually to be a document of almost 4,000 wishes was seen by the arboretum staff as an important archive.

Reading through the wishes you cannot help but get a sense of what it is to be human. Many pleas for world peace, anti war sentiments and requests to respect the environment lie beneath the totality of the document. This is, perhaps, not surprising given that the project took place during a time of global insecurity including the Iraq war.

More startling are the individual requests and petitions for help that cannot fail to provoke sadness and empathy. The list feels true. It inspires laughter with the wishes of children, reminding us of our own childhoods. It also provokes a grin with the personal pleas for help with exams accompanied by an appeal for world peace tacked on as an afterthought. It talks of our struggle to belong and our desire for happiness. It agonises over loves lost or unrequited. It brings us close up to the plight of others trying to deal with the heartbreak of serious illness or the death of a loved one. Above all it reads as a material that is us. A skin that is hopeful in the shadow of our fears, struggles and aspirations. In transcribing the wishes full names have been omitted, but the text remains faithful to what was found on each ribbon.

The Westonbirt wishes are a snap shot of our needs and desires. John Newling is conscious that, for the brief moment that people spent considering their wish or question, they were involved in a moment of reflection. Such moments are rare.

On behalf of John and myself, and the whole Westonbirt team, I would like to thank all the people that, briefly, became part of an extraordinary situation that happened through the summer of 2003.

Sam Wilkinson and John Newling

If Spring Doesn't Come... by John Newling

For Westonbirt, John has created a sculpture in the form of a three-drawer desk containing ribbons. Visitors are invited to write their wishes and questions onto the ribbons, which are then applied to a nearby tree, in time forming a bolus (a ball shaped growth on a tree). It is hoped the bolus will later be cast in bronze and the wishes and questions published in book form.

Before the wishes are applied to the tree we would like to record them in this book. If you have legible handwriting and a few moments to spare please write each wish on the pages provided (one line per wish). At the end of the Festival when the bolus is cast in bronze this book will be used as a reference to create a 'Book of Wishes.'

Thank you in advance for you time and patience.

Cheryl Knight

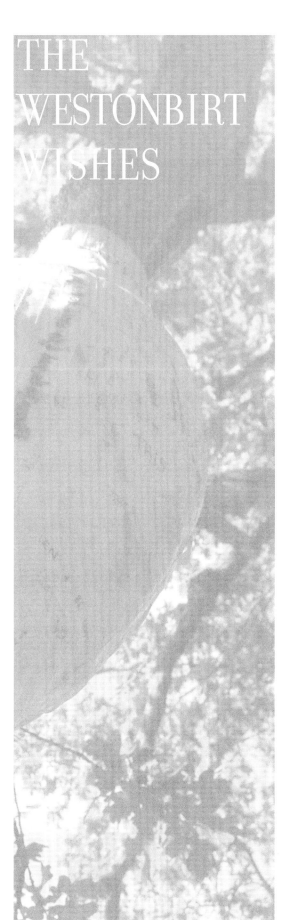

THE WESTONBIRT WISHES

I wish there was peace in the world

Why is war the answer?

I wish we could get rid of all our problems & spend more time enjoying life xx

Lucy to have many brothers and sisters ... & dad to be cured of cancer ...

I wish for an end to famine

I wish people would value nature & tomorrow's resources higher than power and money

Nature will defeat the threats of man

That Emily is always as happy & content as now

I wish I was thin

Why am I doing this?

I wish for health, happiness & a long hot summer

I wish Michelle & I will grow old together

I wish I was a Lego designer

I wish I could get a boxer dog

I wish to see my grandchildren married

I wish I had a big garden

I wish everyone has a nice day

I wish for – every visitor to go away and nurture a tree

I wish I could have a puppy for my 11th birthday on the 11th of July

I wish I had a kitten

Love, only love

May there be peace throughout the world before 2100

We wish for less suffering in the world

For a happy healthy nipper

I wish for Isobel's arthritis to go!

I wish for the opportunities to seek my desires

I wish everyone a Merry Christmas

I wish it were summer all year round

I wish for continual promotion for Plymouth Argyle Football Club – The Green Army

I wish my mum would let me do what I wanted to do

I wish Steve didn't suffer from hay fever!!

I wish my new kidney a long life

For goodness to prevail!

I wish Isabella & cat will get well

I wish four customers to stop whinging at me, and pay on time. Signed a builder

I wish to be with you in May

I wish I was in love

More pleasure from simple things

I wish everyone's wishes come true

I wish I could find a lovely kind intelligent considerate good natured man and have another baby. New daddy wanted

My wish when my time's come I meet all my loved ones again xxxx

May Jen and Nick have a healthy baby

I wish I could stay up all night

I wish our baby to be born well

World peace now!

I wish wishes would come true

I wish my husband was more in tune with nature!

I wish that everyone's birthday is as beautiful as mine is today x

Peace in our hearts

I wish that life was not so complicated, why is it?

Joy for all

I wish I was famous

I wish for a Porsche

Peace of mind

I wish for an increase in the variety of sausages available

That our marriage is long, happy & blessed

Peace of mind – a partner in life – health – long life – children – cats & dogs: I wish for

I wish that we live together for ever

I wish for a healthy and happy Victoria and baby

I wish for strength – strength to get me through the bad times … I wish that the rest of my life to be as happy as it is now xxx

I wish I knew what to write

I wish my night shifts would go quicker!

I wish I could make a living out of something like this?

I wish my goldfish were alive

I wish I had a pay rise & world peace too!

I wish for my husband & I to have a long, happy & fruitful life

I would like to work again

To do well at school

I wish for love to prevail against our common sense. God bless

I wish Westonbirt would never change — let it stay as now — beautiful

I wish the tree team would do more teddy day out picnics

Bristol Rovers to win the FA Cup

I wish a safe, happy & healthy future for my children

I wish they would hurry up and build the skate park in Corsham

I wish my wife could walk again

I wish I could afford to retire and travel

I wish for a baby

May this wonderful place continue to grow and inspire

I wish for this ribbon to be put on a separate branch and flutter in the breeze

I wish I could wake up in a fairy tale castle

I wish that you did not disfigure noble trees by hanging ribbons on them. Ditto!

I wish for success & happiness in London

What came first, the chicken or the egg?

Why did you make such a rubbish garden?

I wish I had a puppy

Money can't buy happiness. I'm happy enough for now, so I wish for loadsamoney!

Make Westonbirt last forever!

To survive OFSTED!

I wish I could receive £5,000 in some happy way to mend my lovely house — please!

I wish everywhere was as beautiful & peaceful as here

I wish wish wish wish, for ever so many wishes I can't find a ribbon long enough

I wish I had a pet hamster

I wish to pass my exams and my Grade 8 violin/I also wish for world peace

I wish to win the lottery

I wish I could see a fairy

I wish for … love and happiness & affection for me
& Mike xx

I wish for a holiday in Hawaii

I wish to find a job that makes me happy & gives me
more time with those I love

May the Church of Christ be filled to bursting point.
Amen

Amelia – a fun filled life!

I wish for Michael to be able to talk

I hope that I (we) will have great great great great
great great great great grandchildren

I wish there was no war no war in the world and to
overcome my dyslexic.

We wish for a long & happy & healthy retirement

I wish I could think of something to write!!*?!!

Health, Wealth (of imagination) & happiness eternally
& love for all forever

For no world wars

I wish people would stop hating each other

Question – now I am getting older should I sell my
bungalow and share another house with my daughter?

I wish I had all the P/S games in the world

I wish my family and I have a life full of happiness &
adventure xxx

I wish to win the lottery

I wish that everyone in the world found happiness

I wish Kai and I will always be happy together

I wish I could fly

I wish tmepen would work better

I wish that my wife and I will be really happy together
and the children will also find true happiness

I wish I had a horse

Dan and Laura wish for happiness together – please!

Peace & good health

Happiness for all that are dear

Bob Dylan plays at the Snooty Fox

I wish Isabella grows up happy & healthy

I wish they would make me redundant

I wish my cancer will disappear

I wish for peace and goodwill to all mankind in my time

I wish I could find love

My wish is, if spring never came, I wish for summer

I wish Bobby to die easily

I wish that my daughters could see the benefit of
sisterly over (eventually)

Peace & joy for all

We wish for lasting peace throughout the world

Are there any flower fairies here?

Why is man obsessed with owning everything?

I wish for continued health & happiness

I wish for peace health & happiness to all mankind

I wish for a long, happy & healthy life for both my son
and myself xxx

I wish for peach throughout the world

I wish love and peace to Thomas and to see you soon

I WISH FOR HEALTH AND HAPPINESS FOR FRIENDS
AND FAMILY

THE ABILITY TO RETIRE

I wish that all this man made clever art stuff would be
banned & people encouraged increasingly to create
bird friendly wild-life gardens

I WISH FOR HEALTH & HAPPINESS IN MY FAMILY PEACE
FOR ALL

I wish for a contented feeling

I wish all the bad and evil is defeated all over the world

Where's Wally?

Peace in this world – learn from the trees

How many forests are being cut down a year?

I wish for a very sunny/hot summer for 2003-
Let's hope it lasts for ever

Why is it that some people hate & kill, when we all
crave love?

I wish good health and fortune to those I love & happy
birthday Paul! xxx

Sam and Joshua Dixon – wish you could be here – all
my love dad xx

I wish for health & happiness for family and friends.

Peace to the world

I wish for Jane to recover forever from her illness

For all my family to be happy in life with good health

Thinking of you: G, A A and R, J and J, B wish you were here

I wish for a more united, caring world

I wish I will see all my family again

I wish for good health for the rest of my days & for my family also

I wish that I will always be happy but also gain £1,000,000 before I'm 55

I wish to win a large premium bond!

I wish for health and happiness for all

I wish for world peace

My special friend is Athley

My special friend is Ellie-May

I wish to gain confidence in Fay and for her to stay safe and well as all my family & friends

I wish patientline would get their act together and do the deal

I wish my lottery number would win to make me happy

How do you know the right path? What are the guidelines? Where are the rules

I wish I could fly right up to the sky – but I can't

I wish to live a happy life

Why does work have to be so stressful?

May the world we live in gain enough wisdom to understand and know the spiritual, emotional and healing prescience of trees and ensure they are part of our landscape for ever

How do's you know who you love? What helps find your souls please in love?

I wish for good luck to all who pursue their life's purpose and to Hamilton House and the Bakery ...??

World peace

My sister Vale lives a long & healthy life, my children have fulfilled lives.

I wish that I could buy an XBox

Health and happiness for all who pass this way

Will every day be like this?

I wish we could be always this happy!

I wish I could stop whining all the time

I wish for a wish and a little wish more

Attchoo! I wish this hanky was a bit wider!!

Happy retirement please with plenty to do

A long and happy life for my grandchildren

I wish for a long and peaceful life for Amelia Scarlett Florence

Love

Peace for the whole world and health & happiness for my family

I wish for a long happy life

I wish for humanity and the planet to be healed xxxx

Wish I knew what 2 wish

Long life, health and happiness for all

Wealth, health, happiness and peace for all

I wish for continual happiness for all

Why?

My wish is for peace – for all of the world

Harmony with me and with joy. Peace and purpose in the world

I wish for once my life would be easier instead of obstacles always being put in the way

I would wish for my leg & back to get better soon

If spring never comes, hope is not lost, the sounds of summer are not a great cost, the seasons may change, turn or retreat, our salvation will be found upon this seat

I wish for the health and happiness of everyone I care about

I wish to be here again in May

I wish I could read the ones at the top of the branch

I wish the gardens looked like gardens & not pseudo art a la the Tate Gallery

Health and happiness for my family x

That Ken & I have a long & happy life

I wish that my wart would go away. Oh and world peace...

What is the answer to the ultimate question

I wish I was happy & content for ever x

A long and fun filled life for Alex

I wish that my children and grandchildren continue to be happy & healthy

Wing nut trees are wonderful – I hope it grows forever

I wish Ben a happy and healthy life

My own health, and that of those I care about

I wish for peace & harmony and a settled family

Why do elderly people I see as a chiropodist always think I am young when I am 36 years old

I wish I could win the jackpot on the lotto tonight

World peace and everyone lives in harmony. No more war! No death and destruction AMEN!

I wish I had blond hair like Isobel

I wish my family health and happiness

I wish Beth's arm was better

For a pet in our family

We wish for a phone call from Thom Champagne. (We have won some money) Given in hope for 2004

I want the bike

I wish to be happy

I wish for a sense of proportion, gratitude, & contentment in my live. Love to all

I wish for a happy & fulfilled life

May harmony sing and all love

Happiness & love

Peace & happiness throughout the planet …

I wish health & happiness for all the family and a peaceful world

I wish for happy times

Health and happiness & peace for everyone

I wish for good health for Emma xxxxx

I wish to be very happy & rich

I wish to be happy

What?

I wish that people would be kind

I wish for everyone to have good health

Love

I would like to see more trees everywhere

I wish for world peace

My special friend is Ellie

World peace

I wish for future happiness for my family

I wish for health happiness and oodles of money to buy a big house and garden to put all these things in

I wish for the tooth fairy to come

I wish for a peaceful tranquil retirement for us & health & happiness for all our family

I wish for my boys Chris and Dan to be healthy & have success in their dreams

I wish that Max grows to be a healthy & happy young man & achieves everything he wants & more

I wish the flowers would forever blossom in the winter

I wish for more of everything good

May this festival prosper & succeed – it has brought much pleasure

I wanna marry Emma. May we both … to many people cherish our love together for ever

I wish my sons Tom & … will have healthy happy children

I wish for universal peace, joy & love, tolerance, harmony & respect, acceptance, honour & truth x

Good health, good friends, loving family – lots of money!

We wish everyone would love and respect trees

PEACE

If wishes were fishes, I wish mine would be caught & would come true

I wish for my children to be healthy & happy always

I wish for happiness for all my family wherever they may be

Love is a precious thing … we get along

I wish every child could have a childhood filled with love and laugher

I wish I had a new pair of legs to walk around the Arboretum

If only the rest of the world was like this, a lover oasis

I would like to come back to be as happy as I am with my husband & my friends

Liverpool to win the treble! Peace & justice for the Palestinians

I wish everyone to be happy

I wish for peace all over the world

I wish that the Biology Graduates 2003 are happy in all they do

When I'm old enough I can play a part in the Harry Potter films

I wish my mum was richer

I wish for all humanity to return to nature & peace for all creatures on the beautiful green earth

I wish I could be content with what I am and have now and not always look to the future

I wish it was always my birthday

I wish I could be rich, famous beautiful & happy & have a family

I wish a professional concert manager would hear me in concert and decide to promote/manage me

I hope my son Jack, will have a happy, healthy & successful life

For my parents to have a happy, pain free & contentness in their final years

I wish that my dream has come true that I will be happy & our families for all eternity

Health & Happiness for Ed & Julia & families ...

I wish that every day could be more like today

I wish for true peace ... to be enjoyed by all mankind

I wish everyone I love was still here today

How many trees make an Arboretum into a forest?

More

Let us let the rest of the natural world ... BE ...

A peaceful year in which memories can unfold without tears and bring mils to all our loved ones. Thinking at the time of our daughter who we remember at this special time and in this special place

WORLD PEACE

What a peaceful beautiful place

I wish to be able to always learn even if there is no answer

How long will it take man to destroy this beautiful planet

For good health and happiness & peaceful times for my family

Bursting from nothingness we see her stars

Peace & prosperity for all on earth

I wish Will finds happiness and fulfilment with life & 2B happy in family

I wish for Martin to be free of pain and for his condition not to deteriorate further

I wish for a cold beer

Will nature be able to always live alongside technology

Peace, happiness & joy – crap ...

I wish for to be very happy with my family and friends, & all to live healthy for a long time together & I wish to have many happy years with Robin, love him lots

I've been granted my wish – I live in Westonbirt

I wish my boyfriend will always be happy & that we love always

Do fairies live at Westonbirt?

Love peace joy happiness to all

I wish the pond was lit

Save plants, eat all the ?

I wish that my children lead a long, happy & healthy life x

For me & my family – peace & contentment – for my great friend, a baby

As many wishes as I want where I want, & I want what I want

I wish my 10 week old grandchild, Amy, a long & prosperous life

I wish for … love, happiness & affections for me and Lisa

For my mosaic to be my financial liberation. For me to be recognised as an artist

Good health for family, husband & friends

I wish to see Max my do again

I am special, so R U …. I am so damn sexy baby

I wish that everyone has a happy healthy life

Please show me a path to follow to find a happy home for all my family

I wish that Phillip & Emma will be together once the pain is over and their hearts have healed. I love you Phillip

Esther wishes for everybody to be nice

I wish for my granddaughter to have a nice friend and for them to stop the bullying

I wish that my life could be fulfilled and happy

I wish we could get rid of the dreadful Government

I wish to marry PJ

I wish for peace health & joy for all my family

Health and happiness for Gilly forever

I wish for my ribbon to hang free in the wind, & not to be bound up in a bolus – thank you

Question; why can't I think of a good wish?

I wish I were a fairy. Lili I wish I were a fairy too

I wish to be free

I wish that my children will always be happy
and content

I wish mum & dad will be happy again & find love

Where shall I use my energy in the next phase of my
life. For the highest good

I wish I'd thought of that & also to win the jackpot

Tranquillity & happiness

I wish we can catch Saddam

I wish that I will be loved & happy forever

For Harry to be happy

I wish for world peas (with my fish & chips)

I wish for the world to be at peace/and my stocks &
shares to rise

How many pork pies does it take to fill my son!?

I wish that I had no nightmares

Phillip Brett Scotcher – marry me!! Love you,
Emma Jane Heatley

I wish life could be as peaceful as this at all times

I ask why I can't think of a question to ask

I wish art wasn't so pretentious

Please make Irene happy

We wish every body would appreciate the beauty
of nature

I wish my daughters and their families long and
happy lives

I wish for health peace & happiness for all my loved
ones, including me

Badgers with guns, really race the world

I wish magic was real

Love is 4 lives, crying is 4 liars

I wish for a happy living world for all

I wish I could be with my boyfriend

I wish that life will lead me to some extraordinary
adventures

I wish for a house in Province

Just to win something to be able to help Joe

One god, one peace

To love & cherish James forever

I wish a happy life for my grandchildren

Love & harmony for mother earth and all her people & creatures

Lily wishes that Belle would stop barking at her reflection

I wish I was a mermaid

I wish for a nice man to come into my life

I wish I could live 'hear'

May the world be a more peaceful place

I wish happiness for all my family

I wish all farmers grew green crops & plants on set-aside

I wish I was in Greenhall Whitley lane

A kind winter to see brother sun to heal the seasons

I wish David Beckham would stay with Manchester United & never leave us – never

I wish to bee 'blossom' in every land

Joshua wishes to find a castle with a beautiful princess x

I wish for a long and happy retirement together

I wish for a new left leg

I wish I was allowed to run about like my big brother

I wish for many more enjoyable years at Westonbirt

How do I have more peace & integrity with Joy?

I wish I could see my 'cousin' and Fran would come and see me more often

I wish I was a princess

My wish is that I recover from breast cancer & will spend a longer healthy life with my family & friends

I wish that I can see my best friend again soon

I wish for good health & happiness

I wish I was a kitten

I wish for another day as happy as the last two

I wish for world domination by me and sharks with 'lazer beams' ...

I wish for health & happiness for all my family

I wish for my mother to be well & happy x

Smile and the world will smile with you

For sun at Glasto, good health for K, C not to change, peace amongst men

I wish that 'flowors' still grow

I wish for world peace

I wish Hannah & Joseph health & happiness

I wish everybody was treated fairly

I wish for Will to find peace & joy again

I wish that my children will never experience loneliness

Eve wishes every one will have fresh food

I wish we find a special place like the Arboretum in our new home in Devon

Beauty is truth and truth beauty?

I wish I could have a third nipple

Why is there war?

I want to be happy

I wish I could see Mickey Mouse every day

I wish everyone would replace the silliness in their lives with love

Health & happiness for my family. Peace in the world

Please can I win the lottery!

I wish for fun, adventure, passion and energy to come into my life

We wish for health & happiness

For peace & harmony

I wish that I could see 'Busted'

I wish for everlasting happiness with the one I love

For the pleasure of enjoying peace with all people of the world

Please for me peace in the world & less hunger

I wish that I could have a tree of my own

Poppy wishes to be a fairy xxx

Will I be famous?

I wish my daughter could recover health soon!

I wish for a companion for my life

I wish to be inspired, surprised & to always live with love, hope, good friends & a happy family

I wish I won the jackpot

Wish you were here!

I wish I would get what I want for my birthday!

I wish I was a fairy

I wish my daughter will get better soon

I wish that I see my best friend soon

A wish that my son Steven is happy

My wish is to create something I'm proud of

Wish for PEACE in the Middle East

I wish Anna to have a wedding

I wish that my partner and her family have a long and happy life

I wish my wishes would come true. Happiness for me and you

Thank you for the peace & beauty of the trees & space at Westonbirt

Wish for happiness & contentment for the rest of my life & my families life

Peace in the world & a cure for all ills

I wish I could be with Phil forever

I wish for good health for my family and myself, and the end of loneliness

I wish that my mum could see this

I wish for a slower pace of life to enable me to just sit back and enjoy – my sons – my husband – my good health

We wish good health and happiness for our families

I wish for Lee to enjoy everlasting comfort & safety – love – to feel the love of the mother he never had

Selfish happiness for me & my kin

I wish for world peace and harmony. PS a new pair of sunglasses

I wish for peace and happiness throughout the world

Long and healthy life

I wish I cold have special powers and I want a nice juicy pork pie!

I wish for world peace and tolerance

I wish that the whole family will be healthy and happy

Peace and happiness

I wish people could life together in peace and support each other unselfishly

I wish Henman would win Wimbledon

For a peaceful true and happy resolution to a human dilemma – Amen

I wish I could love Mummy more

I wish I could think of a wish

I wish the peace we find here could be transferred to the world

For all humanity, a return to innocence

Can I keep this beautiful day forever?

I wish that Sally grows old like her grandma but sees and hears better

I wish for a house in Province with a man I have been married to for 36 years

I wish I had lots of friends

Health and happiness

I wish for a long and happy life for my husband and myself, please make Edwina better

I wish for good health, happiness contentment and good fortune for families and the world

I wish that Matthew could play with me all day and that he will marry me

I wish they would let me listen to my music in the car

Why is my mother so awkward?

Democratically elected Government in the USA

For people to acknowledge the creator of this amazing & mesmerising universe

I wish for all the money in the world

Freedom

Is there any such thing as god? Or just dog?

I wish all the children of the world could see what I have seen today

A lovely place, sweet smelling & cool, another world!

World peace and no hunger would be wonderful

My wish is to continue to be happy & to extend that happiness with a baby next year

Why do we spend so much time pointing out our differences instead of similarities

Happy integrated living with nature, at Yew Tree Farm

I wish I had sidy

I wish for peace in our hearts and minds

What is this life if full of care we have no time to stand and stare

Why!

To make Tony Blair & the government respect the British people's wishes on immigration and referendums & perhaps remember who put him where he is!!

I wish happiness for all the world and we had a nice day

Why – what is the reason for being here?

I wish I could stop wanting a baby and just get on and enjoy life

I wish I could have a tiger

I wish I was quicker at work

A nice bit of land to build my dream house on
(and world peace)

I wish for peace and harmony in the Middle East

I wish wealth, health & happiness for my family

To find happiness and peace of mind

For the kingfisher to return in my dreams

My wish is: my family are happy and settled – that I can enjoy being part of their worlds and every day will not be my last – I wish I could express my deep feelings to someone who would listen & understand me

I wish to have the answer revealed now for the purpose of being

I wish my daughter will soon find a job, a good man and much happiness –and hence leave home DAD

Why does everything revolve around money

I wish England ruled the world again

Good health to my dying day

I wish for a long life and happiness

I wish I could enjoy this peaceful moment forever

I hope Mum and Dad get better soon

To get well, stay well and blossom with more children

I wish wishes came true

I wish everyone to be happy and not hurt

Why?

I wish that everyone's wishes will come true x

I wish and hope my cancer treatment is successful

When the world stops changing so far, will I still be this happy and in love?

I wish for good health & freedom to enjoy it in places such as this

I wish for good health for all my family

I wish for a happy life

I wish everyone was feeling well again

Melissa to achieve her potential

Why?

If God invented man, who invented God?

Peace, health & happiness

Why do I not understand this? Where is my creative side?

I wish everyone finds personal peace & tranquillity here

I ask the Lord 2 look after me and my loving family

I wish for success for my 2 sons as their lives unfold

I wish I lived with Abby Hadsfield

We wish for lasting happiness in France for our family, Miranda, Mike, Piers and William

I wish to have money & health to enjoy more holidays before I die

I wish I could remember my dreams

I wish that people – us, you, me – would take more care of the environment

I wish that my mum stays happy, healthy & doesn't loose her marbles

Long and happy life for all our family and friends

We wish for PEACE in the world

I wish I could have lots of money

I wish I could stay happy for ever

I wish I was a mermaid. I wish I had a cedar tree

That our older years still are years of adventure

I wish that when they build houses they'd plan a wood nearby

I wish to go to art college and pass

We did not inherit the earth from our ancestors but borrowed it from our children

I wish to be a fairy & that this pen would not smudge

I wish this ribbon wasn't synthetic

My love and good wishes I give to everyone

Successful entrepreneurial ideas and activity for me

I wish for a long, happy and exciting life with my loving family

I wish a healthy future for my children

I wish for a better job, I also wish for financial security

I wish that my Grave's disease would get better

I wish Westonbirt's gardens were bigger and more fun

I wish I cold play the piano and flute well and I could have the piano I saw in the Stroud shop

I wish wishes came true: I wish I had all these gardens in my garden

I wish health and happiness

I wish for my mum and dad to get back together and for us to live happily

I wish I could get a highly paid job I was happy with

I wish for our beautiful Alice: may all her wishes come true

I wish the sun will always shine on Westonbirt, the winds will be light, the rains will only be sufficient for good health in the Arboretum

I wish people to share and care for people

I wish that the rain does not ruin the barbeque tonight

I wish people who smoke will stop smoking

I wish I could stop whining all the time

I wish that we could fly

I wish to build a straw bale house

I wish for us all to be happy

I wish we could taste the old apples – they have such wonderful names

I wish for peace, health and happiness for all my friends and family

I wish for health and happiness for my daughters

I wish that Westonbirt may survive forever

I wish for love and strength and peace for my friend FW at the tragic loss of her mother

I wish to have Phoenix back

I wish for fine weather on this spot on 26 July 2003 – all day

I wish that my grandpa didn't die

I wish to be happy, live long and prosper

I wish good health to all people around the world and future happiness to myself

I wish for an end to Muslim fundamentalism

I wish for more flowers to look at; long happy families for all my family

I wish for peace, health, love

I wish a baby for Helen and Franklyn; a long, happy and fulfilled life for Andrew, Helen, Dawn, Franklyn, Jake and Zak, and for all other grandchildren. Peace on earth to all

I wish that I will get better at wirtting

I wish for health and happiness to the Hamilton family

I wish for all wishes to help

I wish to find my new interest/job and Richard will get well

I wish for a happy marriage

I wish I had a star. I wish I didn't have a Sasha

I wish God will live for ever

I wish when I am 18 I could play football

I wish I was married to Thièrry from Arsenal

I wish that I had a real light satchel

What a problem; thank God for the wheelchair

Your wish is my demand

I wish for health, wealth, happiness for all the family

I wish for peace on earth – good will to all men

I wish for everyone to be courageous and to create a thing of beauty

I wish for another 13+ years with Andy – anniversary today

I wish for my dad to get better because he is very ill at the moment

I wish for the girls to have a long, happy and healthy life

I wish for all people in hospital and ill at home to get well

I wish people would turn to Jesus

I wish the world can be at peace as I am among the trees

I wish for my granddaughter, Alex, to one day be able to hear

I wish Nic passes his driving test

I wish we will always be able to appreciate Nature unselfishly

My birthday wish – for my mum to feel better

Why do I have to live with that bloody dog

I wish everyone I love was here at this moment

My wish for Peace in the World that people count not Politicians. That health be restored to Betty and Francis and I win the lottery to enable me to help others

A long and happy life for me and my family

I wish there could be an end to all the unnecessary suffering in the world

To be brave and question everything and then to act

Isaac wishes to fly like a bird in the sky

Thinking of a wonderful boy who sadly died age 16 years old, Jamie Bryant

May there always be places of refreshment and inspiration like this. Thank you!

Peace in the world. Good health & long life

I wish everyones wish comes true. Including mine

I wish that Sue and I will always be together

I have everything except money. So a lottery win would be useful. (I would spend it well and create happiness)

We wish for a dog and a horse and a safe trip home

All could enjoy the gardens here and make their own

Good health for me and my family

Wishing for a long and happy life

Peace to the World

I wish that my husband and I stay healthy and fit to see our 4 grandchildren into adulthood

Give me life to the full

For all children to be loved and safe

A wish for – good health

I wish for long health & happiness

Health, happy life, rich children with good husbands, rest, money

I wish I could stop arguing with my family. And world peace

Nature is the best art. What can we create from it? For own life

I wish for a long happy life of health and wealth. And I wish that my family were happy too

Gabriel wishes a star will fall into a garden

Peace around the World and understanding for all religions & people

I wish to be an actress

I wish that Gary would hurry up and propose. I love HIM x

For here all my love

Lorna and Dave to marry and produce grandchildren & be happy

Sunshine, Water, Love

I wish for more calm, more thought, more care. More gratefulness in the world and for me

Long life to stay happy

I wish that all the people that I love & care for to be happy always xxx

To live as long as the trees

Happiness

Peace and love for all people

Wish for mum to find love & for every person to find 'happiness' in their lives – if only for a second xxx

I wish for my own place in the lush forests – to be closer to and better understand them

I wish everyone could find peace in the world & enjoy the beauty of this place

Why are leaves on trees green in spring?

I wish that everyone could be OK with people loving each other – whoever they are

It's not about who you love – but all about do you love

My wish to meet my future husband soon

No more wars and peaceful co-existence

I wish that I was sure of my own mind

I want to meet Orlando Bloom

I wish to complete my studies quickly and easily (& for Maddy to be happy)

Wish that patience & perseverance did bring progress

I wish for a long and happy life for my Granddaughter & sons

I wish for health and happiness for all

I wish Tom would be really well and healthy

I wish Peace and tranquillity on earth and beyond

I would like to really fall in love and give all of myself to her

I wish for a long and healthy life for us both

I wish for Peace

I wish for world peace good health & happiness & love

I have enjoyed today at Westonbirt

I wish this summer is perfect

I wish happiness for everyone I wish there was peace in the world

Thank you for being here, & for giving us such joy

I wish that this world is still here for my great grandchildren

I wish for good health and a happy life for me & my family

Thank you for the lovely day. May the three of us progress from this day

I wish the immigrants would all go home. Wish the tax was used for GOOD

I wish that my daughter Age 37 will be free from cancer soon

Wishing for a long, happy life

I wish for Westonbirt to receive many more grants & bequests to help maintain the Arboretum & finance an expansion of the collection

A world without wars

I wish I was a better father & husband. Perhaps then I would save my marriage

I wish for world peace. Happiness to all

Good health for all my family

I wish long life & happiness to all my friends & good health for my daughter

I wish for a new baby

I wish for everything in the world to be blue (colour of the sky & soul)

I wish a successful career change to a fulfilling & happy career

Peace, harmony, togetherness for Marha David & me. May time heal & make Marha well & able to realise potential & happiness

I wish for peace health & happiness

Lots of sunshine

I wish to be happy for ever

Everything Gonna be alright from Nottingham

I wish people would not keep expecting me to be on the Internet

I wish for the health & happiness of family & friends

A picnic

I wish that Hester will find happiness & fulfilment

Health & Happiness all round

I wish for a successful career change to a fulfilling & happy career

I wish I had sex with ? tomorrow

I wish I had a 212D

I wish the fairies are hiding in the long grass

I wish all good things last for ever e.g. people, trees, animals

I wish for us to pass each other not as strangers

I wish I could fly like a bird in the sky

I wish that Daisy would live 4 EVA

I wish all humanity would stop abusing & exploiting animals & each other

A long & happy life

I want preying mantises to cover the world ...

I wish to live long & health

For a happy & full life for everyone I care about

I wiz Lee will DXFIX

I wish for peace for all the people of the world

I wish I was rich

I wish I was stronger

I wish I was a shark

I wish I was air to the throne

I wish I was a wreseler

I wish we could live in peace and tranquillity without such noisy neighbours. I wish, I wish, I wish, I wish

Health and Happiness for Family and Friends

Enlightenment for all world Leaders, current and future to work ... for the good, well being of the people of the earth

To live in an Arboretum

I wish that I get to be this happy every day

World Peace – Happiness for All

I wish for West Ham to get promoted back to the Premier League (and Win the Cup)

I wish I was on holiday in Menorca every day of the year

Lots of love xxxx

I wish that my daughter, Kate, became pregnant and a happy mother

I wish that world would realise we all live hear and are all responsible

I wish I lived in the trees and had no coursework and exams

I wish I would go to sea in Florida

We wish for a long and Happy retirement

I wish I go and see my family – soon

I wish I was rich

I wish that the world was made out of smarties
and chocolate

I wish that I'd live here it's a nice place to be

I wish that I had a pony

I wish the people of the world could learn to make a
positive contribution and every day to the world

I wish I could turn stuff into chocolate

I wish for perfect happiness for those who deserve it

I wish to be with Richard happily for ever

I wish for mankind to be as peaceful as this arboretum

I wish my mum and dad were back together

I wish that people lived in harmony and people were
kind and loving

I wish for happiness to come to everyone
(especially Chloe)

I wish everywhere so tranquil

Healing for Viv, peace for Wendy, Joy for Pete,
Love for me

I wish I was a baby

Will he or won't he??

I wish there was no fighting

For peace in the world

I wish Imogen's wish comes true

I have a wish to return here soon

What have the trees seen

May all that visit Westonbirt leave with a piece of
Mother Earth in their hearts

I wish I won the lottery

I wish my son has a wonderful and happy life and
doesn't have my feet

I wish I could speak to animals

I wish all the people in Tetbury come to the festival
of Gardens

Why if the ribbon is so white is the ink so blue

I wish I had a rabbit

I wish I was a shopkeeper

I wish I had a pint of Fosters – Dad

I wish the kids would do as they are told – Mum

Kallum has a wish for everything that is nice

I wish for World Peace

Peace throughout the world

I wish people did not have the need for power over others

Why do people not take responsibility for their actions but prefer to blame others

I wish my son – Martin could have natural tears

Peace starts with me and you. We should all start now

I wish humanity will soon realise it is only part of the world so learn to value natural riches

I wish for a grandchild

Peace, love and ... for the world

I wish the world was a peaceful place

Peace Health Happiness

You've landed in my lifescape and vastly improved the view

I wish for a good and honest lady in my life

May the breezes ever ... free the spirit

I wish and I to ista fuzit

I wish I was rich & erotic clissonal

I wish that Sam was nicer

I wish for good fortune and happiness for me & mine & peace on earth

For happiness and health for all those I love – my greatest wish

I wish it was my birthday soon

I wish I was rich

I wish trees would NOT be cut down!

Happiness & love x

I wish to have another baby. To build our dream house. For lifetime of success and to publish all my books

I wish or hope my wife & baby will be healthy & well, happy & free

I wish the whole world could be as calm & peaceful as a summer's day at Westonbirt ...

How do you put the ribbons on the tree?

I wish we could spend more time at peace among the trees

I wish doc & Tilly would learn to behave themselves on days out like this

I wish there was more laughter

I wish for all my dreams & wishes to come true!

I wish for my tummy to feel better!

I wish I was rich?

A sculpture of a pine cone

I wish Dad got a job

I wish I had a motor bike

I wish my face will get better

I would like to visit this place with my lover, it is
so beautiful

I don't know what to wish for first

I wish for space to do my art

I wish to find happiness, fulfilment and wealth through
my creative talents

I wish trees would talked back when you say something!

We wish these trees will always be here

I wish that I won the lottery

I wish fairies would exist but unfortunately they don't

I wish I could be better at the things that I like

I wish that all humans could learn to live together

I wish for good health, happiness, wealth for all my
family and a little grandson. Keep all my family safe

I wish Donovan would make a decision to move in/or out

For man to love man and nature. Love life and be free

I wish things will stay beautiful forever x

Let us win the Lottery Jackpot

I wish for every human being to be nice to animals and
not eat them and not be cruel

I wish that all of my family remain healthy and content
with life

I wish Anne & I move through life together

I wish for world wide peace

I wish the sun would shine every day

What's for dinner? I wish for steak!

I wish I had MAGIC!!!

Let common sense prevail – for world PEACE

I wish a happy & long life for my children

I wish my mum, dad, brother, uncles & friends all have
a happy life

I wish for all the captured animals to have freedom

I wish I had Magic

My wish is to find what I think I am looking for

I wish my rash would clear up

I wish I would go in years 3 ages

I wish peace & a healthy baby brother

Best things trees, grass, rain, cats, the sea and babies

I wish to be Carin you are lovely

I want to be a princess

I wish that I wouldn't have to put up with my Mum and my Dad

I wish that Abi Stubbs would meet me in Ibiza and we will fall in love forever

I wish that I never stop asking questions

Love & endless happiness for Morwenna & Jan

I wish happiness & Jack sorted

Wish for contentment

I wish I could buy a house again

I wish for peace & Happiness in the world

I wish for a save environment for my children

Pray for John to recover

I wish for peace, health and harmony in the world

Health and happiness for my family

That old chestnut, peace in the world, I wish

I wish for the Arboretum to go on years to come

I wish that the inspiration from today will lead to great design & that I will be a mother one day

I wish to go out

I wish for happy children every happiness

I wish that everyones dreams & ambitions prayers & longings are achieved and everyone discovers themselves in the best possible way. Please keep Rachel strong and stop Dad drinking

I wish this moment would last for ever

I wish that I wouldn't love Scott more than I do

I wish I was a pop star

Twinkle, Twinkle little star forever and I wish I had a little puppy

I hope the sun shines

I wish that I live for today and not tomorrow. Will there be a summer?

I wish I wish that there could be more butterflys & beauty in the world

I wish my Missus was more horny

Jennifer wishes for a magic pony that could fly. I wish I had wings

I wish Sarah had a special friend. Thank you oak tree

I wish purely to be successful in life

I wish for happiness. For true love forever & good health to all the family and friends

To be fearless to be content with all my choices

I wish to live to see my £1 acers grow into wonderful trees

That tomorrow goes well and this job turns out to be everything I need it to be

What noise do butterflies make. I wish there were more ribbons

Why? … ? … ? … Oh, and a new car

I would like to have a never ending supply of free & fabulous shoes

I wish that my brother would always be my best friend

Peace to all

I wish for a pretty garden of my own where I can grow a Japanese maple

I wish I could have two chances at life

I wish that my man would stop shouting

I wish for a big garden one day

Happiness and fulfilment for my daughter

I wish for a piece of land next to my house on which I can grow trees

I become a footballer like David Beckham

I wish my Gran's back gets better so she can enjoy the rest of her life without the pain

I wish I could have a chat with God and hear his answers and a safe peaceful healthy life for all

For my daughter's baby to be born healthy

I wish for sunny days and happiness

We wish for happiness and healthy children

For health and happiness

I wish I had a Gameboy

I want peace in the world I don't want people to be killed

I wish I could fly

I wish I could find peace in myself & that Mike my son lives past 21

I wish time could stand still and we could savour beauty forever

I wish for peace & happiness for all mankind

For Dave I wish you peace while I move forward for both of us sending you all my love under the everlasting sun

I wish that Jennie & I will be happy together forever

I wish the world to be peaceful and stop fighting

I wish for a beautiful garden

I wish that Simon would find love and happiness & get the job

I wish Becky will ride big horses

I wish for calm and gentleness

Sad very sad

I wish for peace & happiness

For a massive lottery win for all my family

Wish – 21 & lottery

Health and happiness for family & friends

I hope I don't die single

I wish for all the animals in the world

I hope me my family & friends have a long & happy life

Winter is over, flowers appear on the earth, the time of the singing of birds has come Song of Songs

I wish my life would be successful and I will live forever and also to be …

Please get our noisy neighbours moved

That the garden's designs continue bringing joy to children as well as adults

I wish their to be peace in the world

I wish for mental stability

I hope my marriage to Samantha George lasts a lifetime with a wonderful family

I wish for us to be in love forever and have a good summer together

To have a happy future

I wish our lives to be happy & healthy and our lives will always be …

I wish I didn't have a problem

I wish health & Happiness to all I know & all who know me

Dragonflies, waterboatmen, an oasis of tranquillity

Is there really the Matrix? Or am I still asleep

Wish Dad's business will improve and prosper

Arborela = gifts to future generations and the planet

I wish my marriage to Jonathan Edmunds on 1 Nov 03
will be a memorable winter

I wish to live in Australia

I wish for yet another roller-tractor

I wish Peter had a better imagination

I wish my Lott plan will work for me

Will it happened and how soon?

Fly me to the moon Sinatra

I wish you would end this exhibition and reduce the
entrance fee

May Neil Young make a new album

Health, happiness and prosperity to all those I love but
always to Brice Erik & Karina

I wish that a talent scout finds me and I star in a
big movie

I wish to be a princess

May my mother's new hearing aid work wonders

I wish for all my wishes to come true. I wish for a dog

Good health for everyone in the family & peace in
the world

I wish for a content quiet happiness for all those I love
(that includes me)

Why did my friend go?

I wish happiness & health for all my family. God bless

May the writer of the green wish have their desire –
for me, my new business to be a success

I want & wish I could go on holiday every Spring to
Spain Greece or Italy

I wish for peace & happiness to come to everyone so
the world will be a better place to live in

I wish for prosperity and abundance

I wish there was peace in the world. I wish people
didn't bully

Happiness & contentment with the man who loves me
for me

I wish for the wars of rage to be banished

I wish to be and all others to be how they want to be

I wish the sun would shine wherever, whatever,
for whoever reads this

Let my future and my love be full of happiness

Where did I leave my hat – any ideas?

I wish that I won £1,000,000

To fly like a bird & swim like a fish and to be a builder

I wish I was a professional footballer

I wish I could do magic

We wish long life health and enough to eat for all who visit here

I wish to be reunited with my mother in heaven

I wish for happiness and contentment in the world

I wish for happiness for my kind family and to spend my life with the girl I now love

I wish that all Mick and Lu's dreams come true

I wish that I had a playstation

I wish to be with Shane for the rest of my life

I want to fall in love

Why do men have to dominate & bully. Life is too short

I wish I could have an ice cream

I wish for a sunny summer Sunday every day

Where is God?

For Julie's cancer to be gone

I wish for all my wishes to come true

I wish for all I love to be protected and Ash to love & be with me forever. I wish to be healthy & prosperous & to win the lottery. Thank mother earth Bo Selecta

I wish I had a garden and – I can be really demanding - south facing

I wish Gordon was real & not just a train

I wish my dad goes to heaven – I wish my son luck & happiness

I wish that everyone was happy & that my Daddy didn't have to go to work

Which is the oldest tree here?

I wish for peace on earth & persona contentment

I wish I will be a football player for Man United & the best defender in the world at age 17 & earn £160,000 a week

Why does a tree have branches?

Cap discriminació ís socielment producivea

Peace in the world

I wish a fairy in the grass wearing a pretty dress

Desso Felicidad para los mios. Todo nos ira bien Papa re amo (none avides)

I wish to get a stunt motorbike

Health Happiness & Prosperity to all

I wish for happiness

I wish for peace & prosperity

Wishing Dave happiness

I wish that the world would grow up

Where is Saddam Hussein?

Where should we live? What should we do?
Where should our friend go to school?

I wish I could visit my cousins

I wish my Teddy would get better and for a house made of Yorkshire pudding

May my two sons better themselves

I wish for happiness for everyone I love, health & the fulfilment of dreams including myself

What is the meaning of life. Canada rules!

Healing happiness, security, growth love peace and a little plot of land to call home

I wish there was peace in the world and I didn't have such a strange brother

I hope Mummy & Daddy get back together again

I wish everyone would stop fighting just for one day

I wish I had a climbing tree in the garden

A mind at rest and a connection to others

I wish to live long enough to see grand children

I wish & hope that my eldest daughter has safe delivery of her first baby in 11 weeks time and my youngest daughter can find peace & happiness after her recent traumas. Thank you

I wish I could have more computer time

I wish for a happy life for all people that they may find a special someone

I wish people would stop letting each other down
P.S. I wish Gordon will ask me to be with him forever

I wish for health and happiness for those I love

I wish I could have an ice cream

I wish I could fly too

Flowers

Good health & happiness for all my family!!!

Let us keep our good health

To keep to my diet & be a size 12!

I wish for health & happiness for me & all my friends
& family (oh & world peace)

Peace, hope & tranquillity

I wish that my throat condition would turn out to be
non life threatening

I wish I was a tree (and a rock star) – question: Do I have
sunstroke? My head hurts

Good health & peace all over the world

I wish for Health & Happiness for those I love
(and 4 me)

I wish Matt never dumps me – Peace, love and
understanding

I wish that Grandpa will come out of hospital soon

A safe delivery. Lissie's dream come true

I wish I had ten wishes a day

That humans will not destroy the earth & will find a way
to live in harmony with nature and wildlife for ever

I wish I will soon be well

All my family lives a happy life (most of the time)

I wish for a happy summer & future especially our
Alps trip

A cure for Stephanie please

A wish that my child may have a child of her own

'Contentment'

I wish for my Daddy to come back

A healthy baby for Sarah & Alfred

Peace, Happiness & Harmony – for all!!

I wish for a long & happy life – Achieve my dreams
& ambitions

I hope that my six month contract @ FCB will become
permanent in London

I wish I had a dog

I wish for a rabbit and a guinea pig

I wish for a house with a garden

I wish for a … world aeroplane

I wish all the poor people will have enough food for
everybody

A long life filled with happiness

If spring never comes I wish I could go t Australia or
New Zealand & live by the beach

I wish

I wish all the poor people will have enough food for
everybody

A long life filled with happiness

If spring never comes I wish I could go to Australia or
New Zealand & live by the beach

I wish for World Peace – and my wife to stop nagging

I wish my granddad gets better because I love him

I wish for a brown dog

I wish for a cake

I wish we find the 'alleged' weapons of mass destruction

I wish to have a fantastic time in Juniors!

I wish that all my family remain healthy & happy

Just a wish to take mum's pain away

I wish people would smile more

I wish all my family health & happiness for the future

Health and happiness for my family

May we be preserved from ever increasing computurism

I wish I could have a baby

I wish for happiness

For my Mum for happiness

I wish Gordon could have seen this garden

I wish to be with Nikki

I wish to be happy

I wish that people would see me for who I really am not
just by what I look like & that I realise my dreams

Have you seen my stick arrow around the arboretum

I wish Debs could keep her house/home 'The Limes'

I wish I knew what to wish

I wish for love peace & Happiness for me and my family

I wish I make a good teacher with a social life! Also that
I get married before I am 30

I wish I could spell better

Imagine there's no countries – (J. Lennon)

I wish for my family & friends to remain happy
& healthy

I wish for the Reactionary Wine Company – Tannin & Acidity Ho!

I also hope that my dear wife can enjoy many years even now she is 75

To meet and marry Nicola

My wish is for a lot more happiness for myself, my son and others

I wish for my own garden

I wish for Cinderella

I wish that I was magical and I had fairies in my room

I wish I could see fairies

What is life?

I wish for world peace, an end to the depression which hangs over the world

Hope, light & prosperity to all. Equality, freedom, liberation & respect. I also wish for personal happiness & fulfilment. My question is: What am I doing here? Can anyone help? Thank you

I wish to get a new job please

I wish for a pet dolphin

I wish I could see my dad again

I wish that Hannah has a safe journey

I wish that there could be more gardens at Westonbirt!

I wish I could be in S Club

I wish every good wish came true – Be Happy

I wish for good AS-Level results

I wish that there could be peace & harmony for all peoples of the earth and that this pen would work

Is God real?

Tree stork Rhubarb

I wish I coud have a swimming pool

I wish 4 Health and happiness for the people I love

Sculptural success Wealth, Health & Happiness 4 Jay

Harmony and love for family and friends – especially Mum

I wish for peace on earth

I wish that I will be able to see Miss Hill & Miss Masuh again

I wish I had a kitten called fluffy I wish I had a metal train!

I wish that people could live together happily without conflict and that plants & animals are treated with the respect they deserve

I wish for eternal wealth and happiness to all my friends & family (+ shitloads of money) please

I hope the world will stay green

I wish to be a famous cyber clothes designer with lots of hardhouse mates! xxx

I wish for lots more trees

What shall I wish for? Health Peace on Earth

I wish for health and happiness for Freddie – with love xx

I wish that Mr Blobby was my friend!

I wish to go to uni with Jai (Boyfriend)

Please help Daddy find work, and love and protect all those we love and cherish … and those we don't

Peace in the world Love one another

I wish to stop wishing I were someone else

Where does art become affectation

Health & Peace for all

I wish everyone would stop taking photographs of the garden

I wish for a world without cancer!

I wish that after Annie's house on Thursday I could sleep over at Emma's house with Annie

I wish for 1,000 wishes and a chick (girlfriend) and a car and a job and a house

I caught a glimpse out of the corner of my eye I turned to look but it was you

Wish Good and long life for Michael, myself and all I love

I wish I have a babby when I am older

Love for us and our friends

Our love will get better and better each year for ever and ever

A Boat

A greater willness for people to welcome diversity rather than judging from narrow perspectives

I wish for peace of mind for all

Be safe, be healthy, be happy. I wish to be loving, loved and brave

I wish I could marry a princess!

I wish for a new job, better pay & therefore a new car & house

I wish there was no suffering

I wish that my mum will have a big birthday

I wish my whole family to be happy

Peace and compassion

I wish everything to stay around as long as the trees

I wish to win a significant amount of money on the lottery so I can buy a house in Australia!

I wish my husband would love me!

To share my happiness and express my love

I wish my dreams for the future will come true

Peace in the world and goodwill

A wish for our Lucy – a full and speedy Recovery

I wish our daughter is successful in obtaining the job she is looking for

Crocodile action man

Is there any frogs in the pond?

I wish I had a god

I wish we (humans) would treat animals & trees with respect instead of trying to control them

Why? What purpose in the suffering – Peace for sand ... & connections

I wish to build my strawbale house

I would wish to be running when I am older because I'm running now

I wish Emma & Stu health, wealth & happiness

I wish that everyone was happy

I wish for a forestry buggy. No war. Disarm nuclear weapons. drop debt

I wish I could live as long as this tree

I wish that all that is beautiful remains beautiful & all that is not beautiful becomes beautiful

I wish for health happiness for my family and to win the lottery

I wish for world peace and to put a stop to discrimination such as racism, etc, so everyone can live happily together

Cinderella dressing up outfit

I wish to live happily and healthly and enjoy my friends' company in a peaceful world I wish for Health & happiness for my family & to win the lottery

I wish for a long happy life & less rain in this summer

I wish we could get along in peace for everyone

I wish I could win the lottery

Why? Does any of it really matter/Is there no fairness in life? Is death better? Why?

I wish someone would do my garden for me, while I make babies

I wish that I had a tree house

Happy family, tree rubbings. Word Peace. Freedom. Joy

I wish for a bit of Peace & Quiet and I wish I would do well at school

I would like a soul mate of mine to arrive sooner than later

I wish mankind to become better at conserving all kinds of woodland. Each of us must do our part. Also health & happiness to friends & family

I wish I was a … & I could spread peace & tranquillity everywhere

I wish I had a tree house all of my own

For peace & harmony in all forms

I wish to know what to write, so that's my question

I wish people weren't stupid

Trees are wonderful & beneficial to mankind. We must look after them. Preserve them for future generations

A safe journey to New Zealand & back

I wish we all had peace

Awareness & kindness for us all

I wish for health & happiness for all my family

I wish that this Tree to be happy

Aly was here – why?

Lord your world is beautiful – let me be beautiful for you. May I know you, serve you live, then live with you in my heart til I meet you in Heaven

We wish for a grandchild

I wish for a happy, healthy baby (and a puppy)

I wish all animals to be treated well

I wish everyone was happy

Wish that Lindsey & Jonathan conceived

To know the joy of being parents. To be a family

I wish for a better use of the ribbons, why smother our wishes – My family stays with me forever. I wish I could have a puppy – good health

I wish I had a puppy. I wish I could go to the moon. I wish I had no homework. I wish I had a big tent. I wish my sisters were very good

I will get every warhammer 48000 model

I wish that I could get a little puppy called spotty

I wish people would stop cutting down rainforests

I wish I could lose weight (me too!)

I wish the chocolate in the shop was free – yum!

I wish Cass would have more chickens and Vicky was cured

I wish for a house with a garden

I hope for everyone to get on

I wish I had a motor scooter

I wish I had a new bear

I wish I didn't wish for what I can't have – and didn't hurt other people in the process

I wish to win the jackpot! THANK YOU

I wish for Peace on Earth, that Anne's memory does not deteriorate so that she is able to enjoy her final years – That I might find God's purpose or all here – That our children may be happy

Why are we here?

Jane & Kerry hope that daughter Sian will exhibit here next year

I wish for a house in the countryside

I wish for lots of money & computer games and computers

I want to wish for climbing frame

No better place than a tree

I wish there was fireworks

My one true love and I to remain lovers in this life and beyond

When I'm an adult can I be an Artist Ballerina and a Mermaid

I hope I'm as well as this tree when I'm his age

I hope daddy gets a job & sees. Thomas the Tank Engine

I wish to be a fireman

I wish I had my own car

I wish I was rich

I wish to climb Mount Everest

I wish you feel the peace of this place. I wish for a bubble gum machine

I wish I could be immortal

I wish there will be no wars

I wish my Premium Bonds come up. Me too!

I wish I had the Lego train

I wish that my life can be happy without chemicals with an extra special man to replace the need for the anti-depressants finding confidence with myself and my abilities

I wish I had a baby sister

May we make the right decision around 1 Oct 2003 – I wish this tree lives another 500 years

I wish for a long & happy life with my partner Clare

I wish for a real garden, how much did this cost?

We wish for health & happiness for our family & friends. I wish my husband was happy

I wish I was a millionaire & had a private jet!!

I wish granddad was better

I wish I was a tree

I wish I could fly on a star

I wish that I could at last find faith and be certain in mind, breast and soul that I believe in was true

Sharing with the poor nations from our wealth is the way to wage war on terrorism

I wish for white:yellow

I wish for a long, happy & healthy life for members of my family

I wish to know what is white

I want to fly – Health & happiness to those who visit this Arboretum

I wish I was popular & had a friend

A brother or sister for Adam please!!!

I wish everyone to be happy – Dad's wish. I wish I had a gardener – to go to Colin's house for lunch

I wish that we grow to be a happy, secure and caring family

I wish that my children will be happy in their future lives

I wish for a peaceful, happy healthy life for my family

I wish Neil would grow up

Health & happiness. Kate being well

To be happy, wealthy & wise. Live long & prosper

I'd like to ride a quad bike and I'd like a batman please Santa – oh and another Bayblack

Wish my brother stop my brother annoying me

I wish to be carefree

I wish Brian could find his way to true happiness & Mavis too – I wish Peter could find a job worthy of his talents

I wish for a microworld aeroplane

I wish my Dad got a job and my mum would be happy. I wish I got a puppy and I wish Mummy got a better job and I wish I can go to Norway with my cousins

I wish there was no litter in this world

I wish for a real garden – How much did it cost?

I wish that I get to see a unicorn and ride one & have a good friendship with it

I hope that Charlie is home when I get back

I wish my family had a dog or cat

I wish I could eat a chocolate bar every day

We shall return to see these beautiful trees again

I wish that people would look after animals a lot better

I wish that my brother Dan have a Winniebago and a motorhome when he is older

I wish I was a horse

I wish I was wiser & hope I do the right thing

I wish for money & to own forbidden planet and peace in the world

I wish for my children to grow up to be safe & happy

I wish that everyone in the world was equal and there was piece everywhere

I wish I could sing

I wish to have SKY TV

I wish I can overcome my fear of spiders

I wish for no more wars and for my cousin to be blessed

Wishing James success in all he does!

That everyone could be kind to each other

Please can I have a real horse

I was in a castle

I wish for happiness & love & peace in the world

Linda – for loves & kisses

I wish that I could fly

I wish for long life and happiness for my children

I wish all three of us to be healthy & happy

I wish we won the lottery

I wish I could fly

I wish to be a Christmas Tree fairy

I wish for PEACE. I wish my Mum will let me have a dog

I wish to play for Newcastle United now

I wish for all ill to be well and not get ill again

I wish I could find a job I enjoy

I wish Kay was here for my birthday xx

When I am grown up I want a big excavator

I wish for

I wish Cecile Brian have a trouble free journey home to Ottowa

I wish for no wars

I wish for peace and happiness in our family life

To find future happiness, love, to share my life with this person, to be able to travel have a family to respect & communicate positively For my dear parents to find peace & realize our love for them

I wish Matt Hawford was my boyfriend, & for lots of money

I wish that I could touch my nose with my tongue

I hope George W Bush doesn't win another Election

Please help those I love to realize how loved they are

I wish all the trees were so tall, especially the Douglas Fir

Get better Daddy

I wish each day could be like today surrounded by beauty & joy

I wish I could go to China & and see the Pandas

I wish that man could accept & love nature and live with it & not against it

I wish for a Happy life

I wish very soon something good will happen for the people of Iraq

I wish I could go to Florida and London

I wish for a new Direction filled with love, joy & prosperity and health

I wish for long, happy, healthy lives for our children

Confiscate Dreams

A wish for both personal and world peace &
understanding

I wish I could find my solitude more pleasing in my
lonely life

I wish that everything will work out alright

Who made God? I wish I had a Pet Cat – I wish a brother

I wish for Cinderella. I wish for a farm. I wish that many
would live without wanting to fight

I wish that I will become an artist, make wonderful
pieces of Art

I wish for Peace in the world. Health for me & my family.
A world of love & joy

I wish for good health & wealth!

Long life, health, happiness, security & comfort

I wish I will get married

I wish I can move in August 2003

I wish to be happy and safe forever

I wish to always know Rose – Peace & quiet

Why can't humans share the worlds resources fairly?

I wish I was Jedi

A life full of fun & adventure

To live long & happy & see children fulfilled & life will
have been worthwhile

I wish to be like a Tree and stop weeing & snoring at night

I wish happiness for all, plus a husband for Heather

The Arms industry to close world wide/ Religion to be
abandoned. Atheism to reign

I hope wished don't stay in the drawer

I wish to be a gymnast & learn gymnastics

Please keep my friends & family healthy & happy.
Especially Dee

I wish, I wish, I wish, I wish I could get a job

I wish there was peace & harmony in the world

I wish being told I have responsibilities and get the
strong feeling I should feel called to the work. I'm a bit
dumb ... I wish it would be made plain to me the nature
of the work I could do

Health & healing for Morgan. Happiness for James &
John. Good luck Elaine in new career

I wish that everyone has a giant garden

I wish there is more gardens

I wish I had my ears pierced

I wish to be good at science

I wish that my friendships will last for times to come especially VYSTYV

I'd like to be able to meditate & find peace

I wish that the world could be much better

The right phone call

I wish for a horsey. I wish to fly on a dragonfly & ride on a pig Me too!

I wish for tom to get better to-morrow

This is a Dream

I wish that my Mum would get better and be happy again – good luck Mummy xx

I wish people would stop fighting each other

I wish for world peace & freedom of speech throughout the world – I do wish for the preservation of beauty spots such as Westonbirt Arboretum

I wish that I could become a doctor in the R>A>F>

Climb a tree – I wish those Martians would go back

Let's hope for equality for all, for everyone to teach potential, to value life

I wish Tony Blair would leave Parliament! I also wish for my Mum's recovery xx

A safe world for all children to grow up in

I wish to find how things connect

A wish for my father's recovery

I wish I had a sister

I wish for an END to cruelty to people & animals everywhere

Why can't Jesus be a folksy dog?

I wish to be thin find the lover of my life and have a family

I wish I could decide what I want to do with my life

I wish for fun & laughter along the way

I lover you place – Olivia. I wish to live happy ever after

I wish that there is PEACE & understanding in the world

I wish we would have lots of snow this winter

I wish I could remember the names of all the wild flowers

I wish that everyone to live forever

I wish that we are happy for a long time

I wish for peace & love in the world

No such thing as being fat

I wish for chocolate

I wish for good health

I wish Morgan Price to return to health soon

I wish for my own puppy

Happiness for my son & daughter

I would like to be free and happy

I wish for Harry back & peace in the world

Do things happen at 12 o'clock at night?

How many trees are there?

Happiness & content in the future for John

I wish that I may find the inspiration & the means to complete my back garden area using ideas gathered here today

A long healthy & peaceful life

I wish to know what I want

To be happy and content with what life gives me & my children

I wish for health, wealth and happiness for all my family & friends

I wish good health for everyone and a wonderful baby for Raj

I wish I could have a real motorbike

I wish I could stop the war

I wish for the best sea ever on Tuesday

I wish that I was a top football player

How many leaves are there here?

I wish for health, wealth & happiness

I wish my sister will find happiness

I hope my granddad doesn't die. I hope my grandma's knee gets better

I wish that there could be world peace and I wish the world was made of chocolate. YUM

I hope that my Daddy will be home in time for my stories

I wish to see my farm again

I wish my brother would be good for ever

I wish we will always be happy & healthy

I wish I lived in a field house in the Cotswolds

I wish to fall in love

I wish for a kitten

I wish that I will grow up to be a good person, have a good job, have a lovely husband & 3 children

I wish I was a millionaire

I wish I won a lottery

That Susan will come home from Australia safely (& stay for good). No country is better than ours

I wish there were enough ribbons

I wish to have an exciting and thrilling life & that everyone's wishes will come true

I wish for real fairy rings

I wish I was magic

I wish I had a pony

I wish for people to accept others for who they are, so we can move forward towards a peaceful world

I wish for Sarah Jane to be able to use her creativity in life & find happiness in all she does

I wish for a safe journey and happiness for all of us

I love my Mum & Dad

Increase the Peace …

I wish for all wars to end

I wish I had a pony

I wish our family live for ever and are safe. Thanks

I wish to be re-imbursed for my … loan to a friend

I wish not to die and family & my friend

I wish to do well in my exams next year

I wish my Mum will let me have a dog

I wish I can have a tree like Kydie and have it as a tree house

My wish is for the whole world to be a peaceful as this beautiful area

I wish for good health for my daughter Lisa

I wish Sara gets his A level results he has worked so hard

I wish Westonbirt could be my garden

Why are all the paintings here rubbish?

I wish loads of excitement and happiness forever in my family and love & joy for everyone

I wish for health for all my family

I wish I had a trilby hat

Second healthy grandchild

Time is everything in this world. I wish more people would use it with care

I wish I could drive a spiderman car which could go invisible. I wish I could be magic

I wish that Bruce loved me

I wish there were lots of ribbons here, so we could write down wishes

I wish I had a dog and lots of animals

Peace & harmony – as here in Westonbirt

I wish that you had a swing

I wish for everyone to be successful & happy

I wish for a baby for my sister & brother-in-law. To show my children as much of the world as I can – I wish for my eldest son to be inspired by school & work hard

I wish I could jump from a plane with a powershout

I wish for success in my life

I wish for my family never to die and my friend Lucy Butcher

I wish I can have a tree

I wish to be fit & my Dad to not bang me

I wish my Dad was still alive

I wish I could stay in the woods sitting in a branch of a Tree

I wish for World Peace

I wish I could have a horse

For everyone to be more tolerant of each other's differences through the world especially of religions

I wish I could have a Norwegian Fiord horse that is …

I wish for love health & happiness for all our family, grandchildren and new baby on the way. So bit it

An interesting turn of mind I'd love to see where the Artist lives

I wish happiness for everyone

Will these gardens be an annual event?

I wish for a successful career & happy children

I wish that I could have long hair and I wish that I could fly and I wish that when I wake up in the morning that I could have a box of spy things

Love, love, love and more love

The bureau sat a short distance away from the tree that had been selected. The magnificence of the tree was countered by the simple industrial form of the bureau. A space was chosen on the trees branch where the volume of wishes would grow as people entered into the transaction of the project.

Detail of the instructions and writing surface of the bureau.
The bureau took the form of a steel table housing a stainless steel collection
cabinet, a repository for ribbons and pens and a simple instruction text.

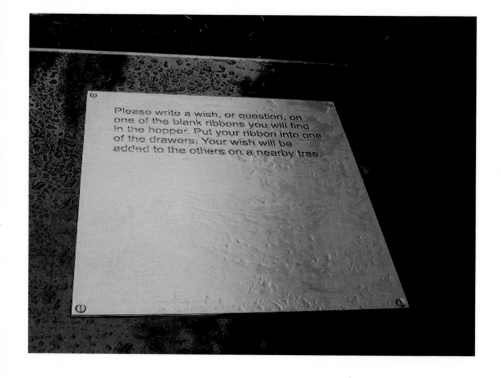

Please write a wish, or question, on
one of the blank ribbons you will find
in the hopper. Put your ribbon into one
of the drawers. Your wish will be
added to the others on a nearby tree.

The ribbons, along with their wishes, were transferred to an adjacent tree.
It was important that the bolus could never damage the tree. The first layer
of ribbons was constructed as a foundation structure upon which the
subsequent layers could be adhered.

Securing the first ribbons to an adjacent tree.
Over the following weeks more and more ribbon was bought and cut.
The Arboretum Tree Team worked tirelessly to ensure the project was
properly maintained.

Ribbon by ribbon the wishes accumulated into a bolus.
Some 4000 ribbons held wishes and questions formed the bolus.

Expert mould maker, Andy Love, began the process
of forming the mould of the bolus.

When the rubber compound had set each half of the mould
was held rigid by a layer of plaster.

Detail of the bolus being separated from the tree.

Once the mould had been removed the bolus was cut away
from the tree to reveal the layers of wishes.
An archeology of human wants.

The final mould.

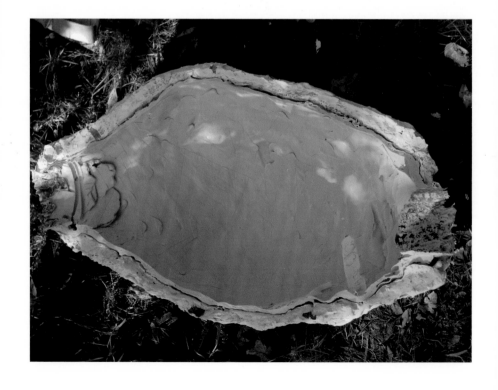

Detail of the bolus material alongside the test cast made
from the mould. A wax skin was then made from the mould.
The wax was then cast in bronze at the foundry.

The cast of the Westonbirt bolus. The Westonbirt Wishes.

I wish for Alice's teddy (Wimpole) to be back from Australia

I wish I was slimmer

I wish to see the beauty in Wendy always

I wish for nothing/no one to injure or kill my family or friends that does not come naturally – Especially my immediate family and especially not my sister

I wish that I could play with a hippo

I wish I could be Tinkerbell

I wish I had a dog or horse

I wish I could be Tinkerbell

I wish that Mr Blobby was my friend

I wish a happy & peaceful life for everyone

I wish I was magic forever

I wish for a good & comfortable retirement for Robert & I

For happiness & fulfilment and health

I wish for a successful career

I need a new lover please

I wish Hannah went away

I wish love & happiness for my children & would like to see more of …

Trev. will be OK

I wish for health & happiness to see my family & friends & that I stop worrying! Also that our wedding day is the best day ever

I wish I could have a candyfloss maker & to win the lottery

I wish that my children have long, happy & healthy lives

To all my family good health wish Li were here by my side God bless

Would that the world will stop over-populating

That we may cope with all life's … & problems with humour & good temper

Peace for the world and love & tolerance amongst all peoples

When someone tries so hard to get something, do they want it when they get there?

I wish that there would be 1 day of Peace around the world

I wish for a place to grow trees – I wish for Julia to meet a really good man

This is a very nice tree but I think you should get rid of the ugly white things wrapped round of the branches. I wish this pen worked better

A red corvette (Little?) Happiness & security for my brothers & sisters

Happiness, health and a little bit of wealth would help

Why are you sticking ribbons to a Tree?

I wish for a healthy happy baby for my unborn child

I wish that Tilly grows to love nature in all its form s

We wish we have a happy time at school

I wish for a happier world for everyone

Jack Bull would like more Beyblades please

Happiness for everyone, whatever it takes! Good health, love, freedom, success, peace, wealth, its up to you !!!

I wish that they could find a cure for cancer. That my Mum will buy me a bra

More ribbons for everyone

I wish for a really good holiday

I wish for Peace. I wish for a new home. I wish for someone to fill your empty space

I wish I could fly

I wish that Vie gets her 'Hello Kitty' wallpaper x

I wish all our family & friends good health & happy lives

I wish my children a happy time at their new schools

For life to sort itself out

Lots of ice cream

I wish for a very healthy & very prosperous life for all my family

Your dreams will come true – good health for me & mine – to be here with good company for ever

I wish pollution will stop. I wish Concorde would keep on flying

I wish to go to Becccarna. Grace gets better from her cancer

I wish we all know how Christ loves us

I wish for happiness

Lots of deep light fluffy snow and clear blue skies for winter

To be no war in my country

I wish for lots of money, big car, big house, lots of land to fly aeroplanes

I wish for some 'Hello Kitty' wallpaper. I wish for a date (or 2!)

I wish for the peace of Westonbirt to spread throughout al the world

I wish the world to be as happy as I

Dear Santa I want to have a present – sad individual

I wish that all my friends are well and are having a nice holiday and look forward to seeing them all again at school

World peace for mankind

For grandchild

I wish I was able to fly

Ellie gets to the school of her choice

I wish that I will win my next gym comp: (all of them)

I wish that clover will live forever with me

For everything to be OK

All happiness for family & friends

I wish I had a Barbie cat

I wish for everyone to be happy

I wish for a healthy & happy family

Happiness for all my family & friends

This project only works if you make sure you don't run out of ribbons!!! I wish next time you would think about this

I wish to feel content and not taken for granted. I am a person not a slave

World peace for all mankind. The end of man's inhumanity to man

I wish to become a successful garden designer

I wish to have a long & successful life

Where is the Bamboo?

That I stay well & Kate is happy

Please may Alan's health improve

I wish for a happier relationship and a stress free future

Enough money to get us out of our current troubles

I wish for better health

Wish Joanne health & Happiness

I wish I had a dog

I wish I had thought of this first

I wish for a rabbit when I get home next to it a pile of money for food & stuff for it and another for stuff for me

I wish that more trees will be planted to make a cleaner future for the world

I wish my son was always good

I wish we had brought some sandwiches

Lucky is the man who can make a living out of footling and pottering around with metal boxes, paper & trees

I wish to be successful & move to France

I wish my son & daughter didn't have hypermobility and my eldest son hasn't got dyslexia

I wish I had a motorbike

I wish for Jack to do well in his exams & for my Dad to realize that a TV in my room is not bad

I wish everyday was as perfect as today

That Kate lives happy ever after

I wish I had lots & lots of cats and had a catwalk for them in the house so that they could travel from room to room

Art! What is it all about?

For inspiration & movement in my work

I wish I had pony

I wish none of my family would never die

I wish I could be a bunny

I wish that I was a feller

I wish I had a remote-controlled helicopter

I wish for health, happiness for all my friends

I wish my grand-daughter's Samantha's & Hannah's wishes could be published

I wish I could be confident & successful

I wish I had another teddy bear and to live forever

I wish people would look after nature

I wish for my own horse

The wishing tree ribbons look like a wasps' next. I wish there would be no more wasps to sting me 'cos it hurts

Somebody to do all the jobs I hate

I wish people one day will live in harmony with Nature

I wish to meet Busted & Kelly

Happiness & health for me & mind

I wish that no stinging nettles would sting me

If there was only one piece of gold in the world, who would find it?

I wish I could get a job

I wish that we may stop fighting each other, no more wars … Disarm

I wish Lindsay was allowed gluten for ever

What happened to happiness? Why is this world full of anger, hatred & despair?

I wish Mrs Fynn turned into a pig …

I wish evrthing is made of white cholote and I'm aloud it

How many beans make 5? Which way is up?

I wish there was ribbon in the hopper

I wish I good at sport

I wish to be rich and happy and to live in a castle

I wish that 2 + 2 = 5!

I wish I had a walkie talkie even though I have one

I wish I could fly

I wish I was sexy

Good health to all my family

I wish it wasn't so easy to make nature look ugly

I wish I could see what this tree looked like without ribbons tied round it

I wish I never suffered from Perthes & that my hip was better

Why are some things in our world not know

I wish that peace would come into the rest of the world while it exists here in abundance

Can we have a baby soon

I wish I could control spring

I wish that my children lead long & happy lives & my son's college course makes him happy

I wish Kerrie will get a job

Man & nature should be in harmony with each other

I wish I will get 1 million pounds a week pocket money

I wish that Bristol City win the Premiership within next 15 yrs. Oh, yea, come on reds

I wish for a pet snail

I wish I was a fairy

A meaningful life

I wish to do well in exams

I wish for my childrens' good health

I wish I had a pony & could look after it

I wish I understood Modern Art 60+ I still trying to get my head around it

I wish that everyone could have the opportunity to experience this place and the chance to experiment with creative designs inspired by it

How long is life?

Good health for all my family

Let Barry & Steve be happily employed

I wish that Cinderella could visit me

To be happy in life and love for ever

I wish Liverpool would win

I would wish the birds would come

I wish my husband wasn't depressed & that I had a proper relationship with him

I wish my boss would realize he is not perfect

I wish that my granddad's body would get better really soon & never be ill

I wish there was some ribbons left to write on

I wish no argument with my sister I get £5 pocket money

I wish that I would lose weight easily

If spring didn't come what a sad place this would be. I would like to be a daffodil & bloom forever tossing my head in the breeze

I wish for a friend who never breaks up with me a sort of giant that never fights with me and come & play with me every day. Thank you

I wish I could go to China & see the Pandas

I wish that I could touch my nose with my tongue

I wish for a horsey. I wish to fly on a dragonfly & ride on a pig. Me too!

I wish that everyone in the world was equal and there was peace & everywhere

I wish I could find a job I enjoy

I wish my family had a dog or cat

Please can I have a real horse

I wish that we are happy for a long time

I wish Morgan Price to return to health soon

I wish school started later

I wish for good health for all my family

I wish I was a skateboarder

Is there a quick way to count how old a tree is?

I wish to know if there is other life in the universe before I die

I hope I become successful in everything I do

VA'RLDSFRED

I wish I could sit next to Dorcas

For sunny days

Will I win the Lottery in a big way

A happy, long life with the best friend ever

Peace throughout the world

Had a Ferrari

I wish that Kate & I can finally be together

I wish for long happy lives for all my family

I wish to weight 9 stones by November

I wish Jonny hadn't pissed on that tree

To buy a garden

That in the future I will have my own horse – Dark boy call Trigga

I wish the family long life & good health

Please let Andrew & Derek be friends again

I wish a pen that worked will come & fish for supper

Can someone invent a Babelfish equivalent. Ta!

I wish I was a fairy

To utilize my spare time usefully

Peace in Africa & the middle East

How many leaves on this tree?

We wish good health & happiness to our family

I wish that harmony & tolerance infects everyone

A hope to grow old as gracefully as a tree

We wish health & happiness to our friends & family

I wish that I had a hamster and a farm when I grow up

I wish ponds never dried up

I wish that we lived in France!

I would the world is better with people loves really deeply, sincerely the others thing say loved

I wish I would understand what the artist is getting at

I wish Clarie, Dean & Daniel lived in Bath

Humanity

I wish my wife a happy day

I wish for an underground den in one of these trees

I wish for Lulu to be united with Bilbo

For continued health, happiness & love of my family & friends

I wish I won the Lottery

I wish I and everybody else in the world could be less selfish

I wish I could have a …

I wish I knew more about trees

I wish for a rabbit

I wish for a Lego airport

I wish that Mum will let me get my lip pierced

May harmony manifest, in my life & the lives of those around me

I wish for the world to be a happy place

I wish to be forever?

I wish I was taller and then I could read others messages

I wish Samuel & Katie would play nicely!

I wish I could fly

I wish I had a bunk bed

I want to be on ENT!!

I wish Lucy will come back to earth one day (me too!)

My wish is for happiness now and in the future

I wish that I will win all my soccer games, and my basketball games

I wish to live by the sea

To have a happy family life

I wish for good health for me & Lionel

I wish that I will find my favourite toy who I lost at the airport

I wish I could be a singer & a vegetarian

I wish my Dad is OK

I wish I knew what to wish for

George wants a hen please

For luck, love & happiness

Sara's wishes – may they all come true?

I wish Teresa and Paul will still be happy

I wish that I had a brother and a sister

Will I find true love? YES

How many times in its life must a tree turn over a new leaf?

I wish to have all the Lords of the Rings films

I wish I/we were millionaire

Please make our house move go smoothly

I wish that I had a boyfriend

I wish I was clever!! (it might be less work)

I wish that soon I will be given a rat. Lots of money for Christmas

I hope that my Mum and dad won't die for a long time

I wish that Clare would learn to sneeze properly rather than sounding like a fog horn! Pretty please

I wish for all the children in the world to laugh a lot

Does this have meaning

People looked after the world

I were rich

I wish the beautiful trees, plants, flowers, and people never die

I wish for all wars to end. And no HUNGER. End the sale of ARMS. Plant more TREES, less CONCRETE

Health, Wealth, & Happiness for all those near & dear

Why's grass green?

What makes rubies red?

I wish I will be loved by you

I wish that I owned a Horse riding stables

I wish that we buy a Sausage dog next week they got on with podge

I want Mike to win the lottery xx

I wish to go swimming

I wish Sarah Collins was nice to me and other horrible people

Nielsan would like a peaceful world

I wish Isobel wasn't such an interfering old goat

I wish for a labrador puppy

Poo

Sylvan & Heather prosper in ther Newfoundland

I wish that someone will bring a blue pen to go with this red one that I have stolen! – Thank you

To meet my ideal man before too long and be happy

I wish to win the lottery before it's too late

I wish it was sunny everyday

I wish happiness to my friends and family

I wish the whole world was a happy place

Rosie to get better please

The Arboretum never dies

I wish for true love

I wish Animals were not hunted

Worldwide Justice

I wish I get a windsurfer

I wish that more people would realize the futility of beliefs and just be

To meet my ideal man & be Happy

Peace in all the World

I wish and hope that my children, and my family will live happy, healthy lives I wish I had a ferret

I wish for my Golden Retriever 'Twister' many long & happy walks in the big Arboretum in the sky

I wish I had a birthday every day

I wish for Super Powers

I wish our daughter Clare a long, happy + healthy Life

Reading through other wishes, I wish that we would all try harder to make our fellow Men Happier, Healthier and wiser Peace and love for all

Why did both car key fobs break the day before we were going on holiday?

I wish for my family to be Happy

I.N. Wish to see. My. Daughter soon

Vote for 'World' Peace

I wish for a happy, long, purposeful and fertile marriage

I love you Guy. That humankind would live and protect our beautiful Planet for our children xxx

Are pets were alive

Why? OH! WHY? Can the world be at Peace

We wish for a fairy and happiness

I wish I was brave enough to do what I want!!

What is the meaning of life and death?

I wish I pass my driving test

To be rich & Happy. No WAR

I wish that me + Bev last 4 ever

I wish for my children to grow up Happy and Healthy, in a world that Values places just like this

Health and Happiness

I wish that my father will come to see me and don't want him being horrible

May the two decide to stay. They are Warmly Welcome!

Please make me well

For Peace and contentment

To get along with different people

I wish my Mum was still alive

If this is a question – What is the Answer

I wish for life to once more become simpler

Poppy wishes for a rose called Poppy!

For Jannie to find the happiness she seeks

I wish I could have a pet

A wish for peace and happiness for all in this world now and forever. And happiness in all of my family

Someone to love who loved me

I wish I could be a mermaid

I wish I had a new job and do GCSE English and Maths

I wish for grandson – healthy & sporty

Madeleine wishes for a giant packet of crisps

I wish my house was made of sweets

For everything to be as peaceful and as beautiful as where I am today

Wish I had land & fulfilling work in NZ

I wish I could come here everyday & play hide & seek in the big trees

I wish for me to learn to love myself and be fulfilled with a loving partner

I wish I could be happy

My wish is for good health for all of us

May Sharan get well again – happy life – friendship

I wish that the world stays environmentally friendly

That all nations whatever religion could live in peace together

Rachel wishes for a Rose called Rachel

I wish I was in a castle

I wish for more hugs and kisses from Cheryl

I wish for world peace and happiness

Desert to blossom like a rose

I wish or my dad to be better

I want to have a baby

All my family and friends will live forever being well

That all the world would be at peace

I wish for everybody to be happy especially my friends & family x

I wish for a lifetime of love & happiness for my children Joseph & Harriet, my husband Chris, all my family & friends

I wish I had a Citroen DS

I wish to have a creative life

I wish everyone could live in peace

I wish to see my son in a happy love relationship

Please keep the limelight mound

I wish that humanity would learn to be in harmony with the natural world no dominating and always staking

I wish my hamster would let me pick her up

I wish women & men were treated equally & given the same pay

I wish to win the lottery

I wish I could get a kitten

I wish for a rabbit

I wish for the biggest ice cream in the world

I wish for health and happiness for my family and friends

I wish that BGS isn't too scary and I do well in school and in the future

I want to be on the lake surfing but it's almost as good here

Peace, harmony, contentment – and retirement

I want a dog

Joy and happiness to all – be happy and healthy Dad

Why are humans so mean

I wish to be a great success as a garden designer

How many leaves are there on this tree – how many stars are there in the sky

I wish I had a horse and that I win the lottery

Wishes for a peaceful and beautiful life together

I wish 4 health and happiness – Thank you

Hope my two boys find their way alright in life & I wish all our health most importantly

I wish I could come here again

I wish for 10 more wishes – please

I wish for a long & happy marriage

We wish mum gets better soon

I wish for my troubles to be OK

I wish for what I already have

I wish I had a game of crash bandacotic 2 gameboy advance

I wish I could meet the right man for me

I hope in the future me & Ian have a baby girl

I wish there will be no more fighting between countries – just peace

I wish I was rich and handsome

I wish peace in this world

I wish for Susan and I go grow old together and be happy always

I wish that all our family have good health, wealth & happiness

I wish for world peace & belief in Jesus

I wish to make a (positive) difference

I wish for lots of love & positivity to come my way

I wish for health wealth & happiness for myself friends & family

I wish I could go in the swimming pool & be a millionaires (not really)

I wish for a happy long life for Stephen

I wish for 'no' tax on my pension

Why do there have to be wars? I wish they would stop

I ask for help with my book, inspiration, guidance

I wish a many splendid thing

I wish for world peace please

I wish that my wishes came true

I wish to be a vet and live a happy life

I wish I got optimus prime

I wish I was the best artist in the world

I wish I was a big massive tree

I wish I was in Wellington

A happy life for all – more concern for the environment

I wish for a army room

I wish for my birthday to be in 1 week and 4 days exactly today

I wish I always went to Aunty Ellen's and played with Will & Dan

I wish Sammy would stop drinking

I wish to be Peter Pan please

I wish that all your wishes come true … so be careful what you wish for

I wish for a cure for Edward (cystic fibrosis)

I wish I had straight teeth

I wish for an exciting & happy future

I wish I could have someone to treasure and adore who would treasure and adore me too

To enjoy myself at school

For joy

I wish for a charming handsome single man to come my way

I wish for a long happy life for me and all my family & friends

Peace in the world

I wish for peace and understanding

I wish there was no school

I wish I was a billionaire & I lived in a mansion

I wish to be content & happy with Mark, Fran & Sam forever

I wish Mum would let me join the Army Cadets

I wish I was one of the garden designers

I wish that Chelsea win the premiership

I wish that everything was made of chocolate

Peace on earth

I wish – please can I win the lottery big

I wish that all my family have a happy healthy wealthy & … life.

Good health & peace for all

I wish I had a dolly

That my efforts may bring results

I wish I could have a 2nd child with Costel –
a brother for Lily

I wish you'd put the common names on the trees!
A beautiful place – great day out

For David and Allyson to be happy

I wish I am a very successful artist

I wish I was the strongest man in the world

I wish I could speak to mom and dad again

A wish for the happiness of my family

I wish the house was tidier

I wish for a charming handsome single man to come
Sam's way

Can I have a larger cheque that £50 Premium Bon win?

I wish that I was the fastest runner in the world. Please

Inner calm. Total happiness and perfect peace

I would like to understand this kind of art!

I wish for enough sponsors to make the Festival an
event forever

In my life make me make the right decision

I wish that I had psychic power and could fly

I wish for peace health & harmony for all families
everywhere

Bring happiness for Sam and Darren and all their
children

I wish for the continued good health of my eldest son

I wish I got going better with Lia

I wish for wealth health & happiness

I wish Stan will be my friend

I wish for love friendship happiness success & fun for all

I wish I could be Tarzan please

I wish for football kit

I wish that my anxiety would stop

I wish for Emie to get better

Health happiness wholeness deeper spiritual
understanding

I wish for my own bedroom

World peace

I would like to have all the Lego in the world

I wish for peace and goodwill to all human beings

I wish the Oil Col would send me a bill

People to live in peace everywhere

I wish for the world to be kept clean for me

I wish I could swim with Dolphins and be a teacher
when I'm older

I wish I had a good job

Peace between nations

I wish the Autumn colours to come early

I wish my school world burn down

I wish it was easier to find the exit or this place to close

I wish that Sarah finds true happiness

I wish I had a pony

I wish for the sugar planet toy – Xmas

I wish for a happy and healthy future

I wish that people learn to love & respect trees and the
planet again becomes covered in trees

I wish for Ralph & the baby & I to live happily ever after

I wish that Martin Canning will go out with me

I wish for both myself & Jessica to be happy & Healthy
all our lives

I wish I had a cat

I wish I was a tiny grub with hairs around my tummy,
I'd crawl into a honey pot to make my gummy gummy

World peace in our time

Everlasting serenity

I wish for a playmobil

For Aonain to live again

I wish Andy will be OK after his operation

I wish to fall in love

I wish everyone was happy in the world

I wish that my niece grows up to be a happy woman

I wish for Ossie, Blain, Gareth & Helen to be at peace
with themselves & with us

That my brothers find happiness as I have done

I wish for bright sunny days filled with love & REIKI for
all my friends & family

What is the meaing of it all. P.S. I like your work
thank you

I wish my memories last on

Wish the ribbons had been hung separately – it would
look beautiful

Why are there so many tree species?

Wish the Act of Synod relating to Women Priests had
not been passed

I wish I was a dragon

We wish that the beauty of Westonbirt could be reflected
across the world

I wish that no child in the world grows up in poverty

I wish for another owly (Tawny Daughter)

Please find a cure for cancer + any other ailments

Wishing Nick a speedy and successful finish

For an Action Man

I wish I had a back garden like this

I wish I find true love

I kill all knob munching gekkos Ta very much

I wish for wife to be healthy for the next 50 years,
especially in the next week

I wish for my children to live long, happy & peaceful
lives & for the world they live in to be safe & united in
peace

I wish the peace of this place could fill the world

I wish to stay happy, healthy & fortunate for many
years to come

I wish for health & happiness for all my family

I wish bananas would grow on trees

Gayle gets well and granted her 'dream'. Kiera finds
peace, and the Lord looks after this peaceful and
beautiful place

How can we learn to live in peace

I wish for harmony … in all things

Wish for health & happiness for all my family

I wish for a jolly tall (Giraffe)

Good health with love happiness & creativity

Being good

I wish for good to triumph over evil

I wish 4 fair trade across the world

I wish no-one I know gets ill or die xx

I wish that me & Adam live a long & happy life together

I wish for peaceful earth which people can enjoy forever
& I wish to marry Kerry Sambells

I wish to have a happy future which is full of love!

I wish for a fantastic Glasonbury '04 with U2 headlining
and to be there with all the people I love

I wish that everyone who is in need of peace can
experience the tranquillity of this Arboretum

I wish I win the Loot big

Many happy returns of the day

I wish you don't die from Gonodeyma, but grow over it
and become 6000 years

I wish to have a Harry Potter toy and lots of little ponies

To be happy and content

I wish the weather would buck its ideas up

I wish for a bright kitchen filled with good food, good
health, the love of my life, children and very friendly
pets

A wish for peace, health and contentment – so leave
me alone!

Peace in the world, health happiness, improvement in
cash flow

Health

I wish for happy healthy lives for my family. Thank you

Wish for a bouncy castle

My own health, and that of those I care about

W H Y?

I wish I had an elefant in my gardun

I WISH FOR PLAYMOBILE FOR MY BIRTHDAY PLEASE

I WISH FOR HEALTH AND A FARM

I WISH NATURE NEVER DIES!

For another hamster

A happy and honest live wherever it may take me

I wish I could live closer to nature – maybe a ti-pi?
I can't spell it

My wish would be for more income and less expenditure.
Peace in the world

I wish the thrushes would come back to my garden

What goes up a hill with 3 legs and comes down with 4?

I wish that my children's health will be good 4 the rest
of their life's

I wish I could live always amongst such peace and beauty

I wish that one day I shall learn to walk again

I wish I still believed in Santa Clause

LOVE

Understanding

I wish for a bouncy castle

I wish for love & contentment. Good health for my friends

Will Matt ever sell his bloody house?

For special food

To be able to always walk and see such beauty

I wish Tony would come to his senses! What a silly boy!!

I wish for peace and serenity

I wish my unborn child is well & all my children forever happy

I wish my friend played with me!

I wish for a grandchild

I wish Mum & Dad are never lonely and sad – but always happy

I wish that I will become rich and famous because I know that I have the support of my friends & family

I wish the war would end between Iraq and England/America XX

My children get their lives sorted soon

I wish for peace and happiness for my daughter, son & grandsons

Please keep planting trees – all types – they are dying too quickly

I wish to be somebody

I wish my baby to be healthy

I wish it could always be as peaceful and lovely as it is here today

I wish they would make me redundant

I wish for a really big climbing tree

I wish for peace happiness and tranquillity

I wish thease fly's would – off! And my hair would grow back

I wish for more model trains. Get rid of asma

I wish no one lived in poverty without food or water or fear

I wish as many more years of joy as today

I wish for Peace, Health and Happiness

But does the tree mind?

I wish that Katie finds a boyfriend who is kind to her
and makes her laugh

Why are the rhodendrons gone?

I wish for world peace and happiness forever

I wish for a trampoline Keanu Reeves 4 my mummy

How long, o Lord, How Long!

Remember thy Creator in the days of your youth –
and always

I wish wholeness and happiness 4 Mark

Let me find happiness, love and peace – let there
be light

My wish is for health, and happiness for Andrew and
Natalie who both suffer too much

I wish everyone could touch a hundred year old tree
every day

I wish that my Mother realises how special she is

I wish I was a tooth fairy

I wish to feel well all the time

I wish the labels on the trees were more visible and
bigger

I wish we could come to Westonbirt every day

I wish we would take the peace, tranquillity and beauty
of the trees into our offices, homes, shopping centres
and roads

Which came first, the chicken or the egg?

End any war

Happiness and a safe world for Daniel, Emma, Sally,
Kiernan & Kelsy

I wish for health, happiness and peace for all of the
world and its people

I wish for Happiness & serenity like Cornwall. I wish to
live in Cornwall

I wish my hair colour was so, so, so, so, so dark

Why does every bad thing happen to me?

I wish mankind would learn from Nature

I wish for joy good health – no more, no less

Peace in Palestine for future children

More please, less mobiles!

I wish for my children to have a happy, healthy, safe future in a peaceful world

I wish for love & happiness for our son Seth

I wish for more of what there's less of & less of what there's more of!!!

I wish Rob is my dad

I wish I could be a mother

I wish that Luke had a building-clock castle so that we could play with it together

Please no killing thanks

I wish I was famous & rich …

I wish 4 & I Z marry

I wish to enjoy life

I wish that all the boys thought I was fit! And I get re-picked into the AB team PLEASE

Heath Wealth & happiness

I wish for my friends & family to remain happy & healthy

My wish is for a lot more happiness for myself, my son and others

I also hope that my dear wife can enjoy many years even though she is 75

All my family lives a happy life (most of the time!!!!)

I wish that I find a loving, caring man to compliment my life

I wish to have a special & happy wedding on August 30th 2003

Good weather in the N.E

I want a lollipop

I hope to be able to come here till one day I die.
I am 75 now

We wish to live happily together for the rest of our lives

All war to B ended!

Alexander wishes for a car

Working by Christmas

I wish that my Dada and mummy whould learn to change and yet fit

Wish that more orchards could be retained in our country

Long live British Forestry

I wish for Liz & tom to have a baby soon

BJP wishes for a fairly long continuation of his life in a healthy and happy state

I wish I coude red

To be real tinkerbell

I wish I could live forever. Ps Jesus name amen I wish for the health and happiness of all & that all children are given wonderful and safe childhoods that lead to a better future for everyone

Food for all mankind. Bread not bombs

Why are gherkins so disgusting?

Load of old bolloks

I wish for completion, for peace, for seeing its all

I wish for lots of summers like this one (2003)

I wish that I could go to Spain

I wish my garden would bet bigger

I have always wished there to be more birds singing

Why can't all families be as happy as ours?

Yes, for a coalition between nature and humanity, but at the same time for coalition between human beings

I wish she was pg

I wish for A Princess Barbie

I wish I was immortal

I wish I can be like an oak and live forever so I can always look at the trees in the Arboretum

I wish happiness & peace for Christina

I wish Wilson will live to a ripe old age

I wish I had a sister as well as a brother

I wish that I find £100 today in an envelope Why can't I think of a wish? Is there too many things I want or not enough

I wish to get into BRGS

I wish for KDF to stay well forever

I wish for my daughters to be happy and successful

I wish for old friendships to return unmarred and unmarked by new acquaintances

I wish that my cancer does not come back

Harry (aged 4) wishes to have something to eat

For the Arboretum & Silver wood to remain a place of peace and tranquillity

I wish I could see my Dad again

How are ribbons attached to the tree?

I wish I had £100 today

Why can't I live in Skye?

I wish the ribbons could dangle from the tree

I wish Dad gets better soon

I wish for my family health and a long life

I wish that the holidays lasted for ever

Peace all over the world

I wish that I was young again

I wish that the world could be as peaceful as it is here

I wish that I could make a wish without my nosey family looking at it

I wish for a mega sword

I wish for my daughter's wish to come true

Peace in the Middle East stop the killing

I wish happiness for my daughter

Peace & Happiness for everyone

I wish that there was a playground here

I wish for my family friends, fiancée and I live long safe happy and fulfilled lives

I wish that the family would get back together

I wish my parents would come back to live in England

I hope my battery doesn't run out

I wish for a new big teddy

To have lots of money

To own this fantastic tree. I wish to become the best … in Britain

I wish that I was brave enough to pack work in and open party animals business

I wish all the wars stop

I wish for a money tree to help the poor

I would like to know how to make my garden grow

I wish I didn't have to go back to school!!

I wish for a peaceful 2004 around the world and a happy home in Tetbury for my family

I wish my daughters & family have a happy & healthy long life – and that the planners don't come!!

I wish for peace, green space and a new home 4 Keith

Where did I leave my glasses?

Long healthy life for Westonbirt Arboretum

I wish I can live 1000 years please

Georgina wishes for a spaceship

For everyone to find peace and tranquillity daily

I wish I colde talc to animls

I wish everyone would have faith in JESUS CHRIST

World Peace

High and Grandma wish to go to the moon in a spaceship

I wish for contentment for what we have & pleasure in life

Mummy needs to chill-out and not tightly wrapped

I wish that I never have to leave mum and dad

How old is the tree

Hugh and Eduin will always be happy & good

Again next year!!

I wish that there could be less distance between chaos & creativity

I wish for the happiness of my daughter. Find love Ruth!

Love & a happy life for Thomas, Tiggy & Sake

I wish for all sins to be forgotten

I wish for the world could be a more peaceful place

I wish that world was as harmonious as here

I wish for a cure for cancer – for George

I wish for life in full health

I wish to live to see my children grow up, marry and be happy

I would like the Arboretum to still be here in 40 years time and to be physically able to return here then

I wish for peace in the world

We are rushing towards … what? Why rush?

Good health to all my family

I wish for the happiness of my family and the fertility of my friends

I wish I was the best footballer in the world

I want to be happy …

I wish I could have a nice dog

I wish more h

I wish for a Barbie aeroplane

I wish for peace

I wish I was a goød. You spelt this wrongly but never mind perhaps you will get gooder

I wish for Grandad to get better soon

What is the meaning of life, the universe and everything in it?

I wish I had bunk beds

Love, health, wealth & happiness for Paul & Sally, dear friends

A life of contentment and happiness

An end to wars – and evil

A wish for creativity & Blessing

Clare & Shaun Wilde Walker Molyneuse wish to live happily & in love for ever after

I wish to have a fountain in our garden

My wish for peace. For everybody to live a life they would be proud of displayed on their tombstone (epitaph). God Bless this beautiful place

I wish for endless love

I wish for peace and goodwill to all humanity

We hope and pray trees will always dress the countryside and add colour to a sometimes drab world.

For Dad's operation to go well

Please keep the Limelight mound

I wish for Charlotte and Phoebe a long and healthy life

50 years ago I came here and now I know why, Perfect Peace. I have long wanted to come back

To wish health and happiness to all our Family

How many wishes are on this tree

I wish for Melanie's hair to grow back, and that they get their house

I wish that Leicester City FC will win the 03/04 League

I wish to win the lottery and have good health

I wish that Tony Blair would stay in Tuscany

I wish that the world was made of chocolate

I wish for happiness and a tree filled world

I wish all wishes would come true

I wish I had a pet horse

I wish that there would be no more wars

I wish I was famous

Less concrete, more trees

Win the lottery

That this place always exists

I wish I would get bigger

I wish I could have a beagle before I'm 14

For health and happiness for my family & Friends

Health and wealth for all

I wish to be with Carl again

I wish I was a gymnast

I wish for my father's release from his agonies.
Please God

I wish for peace on earth

Happy, happy life for Holly, Ben and Tom

We would wish Charlotte to eat her meat so she go
to Disney

I wish for all my children's good health and happiness

I wish to be pg!

That the world would be more tolerant and that peace
would come before war

I wish for happiness, success, good kids and a bit of
cash!

I wish that I have a horse

May all people on this earth live at peace with one
another

Dan & me – happy together for ever

William wishes for a puppy

What is the point?

I wish Dave and I are happy for ever

I wish everyones wishes for good to come true

I wish my family happy days

All people of the world to experience joy and
happiness in their lives

I wish I had a lobster

Eternal happiness for all

I wish for a guinea pig

I wish there was no school – who needs education

Rosie & Molly wish for a Barbie & to be happy 4 ever

I wish Jonathan and me are happy with our new life

My family to be safe & find peace & happiness now
& forever

I wish I was famous

Happiness, health & Peace of mind

I wish to grow old and wise, just like an oak tree

I wish I don't get told off in the Juniors

We all get what we wish for

I wish I could swim with dolphins

I wish for a big tree in my own garden

I wish I was a bilionair

I wish I was a billionair

I wish that my mother gets well again and finds peace

I want to be a super sayan

I wish for myself, Tom, Dave & my family to have good health & be happy. To have wealth in abundance in order to achieve our dreams & goals in this lifetime

Brandon wishes he will be very rich (aged 5) Daddy wishes Brandon would suddenly become very sensible. Mummy wishes she will be very happy

I wish for Bonnie's leg harness treatment to be a total success

I wish my Dad was …

I wish for more McDonalds

I wish for all people to be content

Why is there so much greed in the World?

May all your wishes come true – our wish is this

Return of my Youth

I wish for Tottenham Hotspur Football Club to do well this season

I wish for Mari to settle into Bristol and our flat well and with ease

I wish to have a happy life together with Christine Jane and Thomas. A fun wedding on the Sunday before May Bank Holiday. A lovely house which we all grow together in harmony. Ps. All holidays are fun holidays

I wish to be able to enjoy the trees & wonders of nature for years to come

I wish Westonbirt Arboretum Tree Family all they wish themselves

Terry – let go lightly – my love goes with you x

I wish I had a horse

I wish for a husband who will take care of me

I wish for happiness for myself and everybody whose life is tough

I wish for eternal life in paradise for everyone with perfect health and happiness for ever. Praise Jah forever

I wish I had a baby brother

I wish we could live in Scotland soon & forever. Just Joey & me

I wish for health & happiness for all my family

I wish for a super holiday for us all

Who am I?

How many different greens

I wish I will follow the correct path in life

I wish for a football kit

We want to win the lottery

Why is the world full of war when we are all in the challenge of life together

I wish all my days at school to be fun

To be a mum

I wish that I could do better in school and to work much harder in year 5 than I did in year 4

When is it going to come. You will know what it is when the times comes

I wish for a kitten

I wish I was preggers!

To get well from my cancer and meet my man

I wish for love peace & charity to being my hopes, ambitions, dreams to fruition

I wish for world peace

When will Miss Barlow be back

I wish my handsome prince would enter my life & whisk me off to faraway places

Just why is Westonbirt so wonderful!

I wish for a baby

I wish the newspapers weren't so critical of the government

I wish for good health

I wish for a spiderman costume

How do you become a Professor in Installation Art

Please keep Limelight and the Homage

I wish for health, happiness & love

I wish all my days at school to be fun

I wish my daughter's happiness

Does life matter? What am I? Is there such a thing as happiness?

I wish for a moment in time

I wish for a cat

I wish for peace in Israel/Palestine

Creativity – Life

I wish for love and peace in this world

I wish for hope and happiness

I wish that wishes come true

I wish for an Autumn as beautiful as the Summer

May S find a partner and family

I pray for peace in my life and untold happiness – Amen

I love Daddy

I wish I could fly

I wish for a dog

I wish Clare could see this tree, she probably can!

I wish this tree would last forever

I wish for all the bunny rabbits to stay away from Mr Bacon and Rolf Harris, and for all the trees to grow old and die happy. P.S. Great sculpture! (You'd never find one like it in IKEA!)

Good health

My wish is for mankind to consider that he is part of nature

I wish for happiness in life

The world to live in harmony with nature

I wish for peace in the Middle East – We'll need all the prayers we can get

I wish for no nasty surprises

I wish that mankind learns to respect and conserve the environment

Plant many trees

For love to be made law

I wish I had more wishes

I wish that the Purdoms & Couves meet up again soon for another picnic

Urit will be happy and full of love

I wish for Charlotte, William and Robyn love, laughter & happiness on all their days

I wish I could turn back time to perfect the mistakes
I really regret

I wish for world peace and tranquillity throughout
the land

Will I angle in my rest?

I hope I have lots of sun on holiday 'cos I'm on holiday

I wish I could have a secret den

I wish for long, happy lives for my family & friends

To find a place to live

I wish to do well & earn more money

I wish for the external peace of trees

That all nature & humans can live together in peace &
tranquillity & harmony

I wish Gabi was well again

I wish that the world will grow many more trees to help
save our planet

Sometimes the more you think there more there is no
real answer

I wish for Tranquillity of my soul, & the wisdom to see
what others need

Wish for peace & friendship in the world

I wish I could see the bamboo

For strength for our family

I wish for proper gardens next year

I wish to grow old and in love with Henry ...

I wish I become an actor

What shall we do when we retire?

I wish for what only I know

Wishing for goodwill & happiness in life's journey

I wish that religion didn't start war as we can believe in
who we want!

I wish the people I care about would be happy

Where can I buy the DVD of Fifteen Stories High?

Health & Happiness

I wish for a thousand pounds

I wish I could come here more often!

I hope & wish to win the lottery & plant lots of trees &
have a beautiful garden

Love and Good Health

The end of religious bigotry & fundamentalism! PLEASE

I wish for health & happiness for all my family

I wish that everyone will find happiness & fortune in the future (& get a d.o.g.!!) xx

Please, rest & fulfilment to my soul

Please being Emily back my best friend

I wish for love and happiness to triumph over war and destruction

PEACE

I wish that all of Guy's problems be solved

I wish I knew what to do

Why oh Why oh Why oh Why oh Why oh Why oh Why oh Why oh Why oh Why?!

I wish next year to be a happy one

I wish for a way out

Why doesn't everyone like the rain?

I wish that soon my husband gets a good job

Abundance Please, in health, wealth & happiness

I wish for Peace & Harmony on this Earth

Love me?

I wish I could have a horse

Why is Jennie going to go away and close the bookshop?

I wish there was a bit of respect for this tree

Wish for peace in the world

When were the sweet chestnuts planted?

How old is the tree?

I wish for a long & happy life for my children

Hope arboretums live for ever

I wish that my family & friends will be safe & healthy

I wish for world peace

'Man is that he might have joy'

May the force be with you!!!

If pigs could fly … anything could happen … if only …

I wish to win millions

I wish for peace in this world!

I wish for my family to live happily ever after

I wish for health and a new lease of life

I wish … there can be more true love in the world

Let me help the world & Africa & keep my family safe

Love for All

Good health for my parents

I wish Peter would ask me to marry him

I wish I had a horse and a foal for Adam

I wish … to learn to love myself and others more each day x

I truly wish to find my creative destiny – Thank you

Please bring Peace to the world

I for world Peace

I wish to be with my true love for the rest of my life

I wish I could see and be friends with a fairy

A long happy life of wedded bliss for daughter Claire

I wish for a wonderfully happy existence where I am surrounded by beauty and people understand me for me – Thank you Tree

For my children to be happy and healthy

I wish I was a tree

Please can I have a place to live where Briony and I are happy. Not told what to do and that I can afford comfortably. Thank you

I wish for a happy long life x

I wish the house was finished

I wish for my job to be sorted out

I wish we had Disney channel wish I had a …

What came first the chicken or the egg?

I wish the world could be as peaceful as a tree

I wish everyone would plant a tree

Health – what else is there to ask for?

I wish to pass my MA

Is Lancashire really the centre of the universe?

I wish I had more plants than 100

I wish I knew what to wish for

I wish summer would last for ever (and the cricket) x

I wish I had a puppy or a rabbit

The people will shut up

I wish I can have a limosuine for my birthday party

I would like to know what the tree is

Fly fairy fly

I wish for a happy family

I wish that every man acknowledged God as Lord and could love him more than self

I wish I could sell my house and move home to Dorset. Also a small lottery win would be nice. Thank you

Retire soon – Long life

I wish a happy and healthy life for my children Claire, Charlotte and Lindsey, grandchildren Jaime & Adam

Is Blair really sane?

I wish for lovely holidays

I wish for everyone to have three more wishes

Peace and a long healthy retirement

I wish for happiness and peace in the world. I wish for happy endings and fresh beginnings. I wish for harmony to replace dischord. For me I wish for lasting love and friendships

I wish for a better job

I wish long life to all Arboretum, all trees and all couples married this year

I wish I could have a glass screen

Wishing for a full recovery

Wishing for McDonalds to go Bust!

To be a Bolus

To marry the most handsome fun man and never be sad again

Sally for loads of smiles and happy carefree life – she deserves it

For me & my family to get a break, no more debts, no more trouble – just to be happy & free

Will we wait forever?

Pray folk will find the tree where eternal life was won

I want my family to stop nagging me, then I won't have to tell them to shut up

I wish to return

I wish Harriet could be my twin because we are best friends

Happiness!

Stop bickering and get on with it please

Health & happiness to my family

What is the meaning of life?

I hope that branch won't break, & peace for the world

Jordan wishes for a train

I never got into trouble

Respect everything

For lots of money

When I am older I am as good as Jason Robinson at rugby

Quo vadis

Love ... peace ... understanding ... wisdom ... happiness ... health ... honesty

Reading F.C. to be promoted & have at least one year in the premiership

I wish I was a millionaire

I wish health and happiness to all

I wish for regular bowel movements

No wishes anymore, just grief and love. Forever

I wish I was a tree

I wish I could go on holiday for a very long time

I wish to go on safari

I wish I was an inventor

I wish for health and happiness for all my children

If money doesn't grow on tree, why do banks have branches?

Oh for a fragrance

I wish I was a zoo keeper

I wish to see my friends

I wish peace and happiness to all

I wish all bad things go away

I wish to be good at football

I wish we can stay together forever – and live in the country with a little Jack Russell called Nipper – always together

I wish to go beyond ...

I wish for there to be an end to death

I like the trees and forest and the gardens esp. the snake in the grass and the red bench

I wish that next year's garden festival is as good as last year's

I wish to have a PS2

I wish I was sexy

Where is the tomato sauce?

I wish to be well

I wish no more kidney stones

I wish to have a dog for Christmas

I wish health for my family and me

I wish I had a pet rabbit

Let beauty and peace be our guiding lights

I wish to go to lots of parties

I wish I was a lifeguard

I wish for Ricki to be happy

I wish for a long and fulfilled life

I wish I could find a soul mate to share my life,
my thoughts, my love, my interests

I wish that Kate and Mike sell the house soon

I wish that every child could be free to enjoy their
childhood years

I wish happiness for my friends and family

I wish happiness

I wish Angelte to get better quickly

I wish Anne could have a happier life

I wish I had a stereo

I wish the tree was normal ie no silly bandage!

I wish I could leave. This is not boring but I don't like
getting wet

I wish for peace, health and well being for all my
family, friends and me

I wish that one day we can live in the country and that
Jason will marry me

I wish to move to New Zealand – for good

I wish I had a helicopter

I wish for health and happiness for friends & family

I wish for determination to cope with problems real
or imagined

I wish the tree has another bandage over the pond

I wish for good luck – the rest I want to do myself

I wish that soon Jacob will find a good pathway in life

I wish I was 25

I wish to see and be with the stars

I wish I had a brain

I wish for a motorbike

I wish for lots of money

Ella wishes for her teeth

I wish I had a mobile

I wish that world lived happy ever after

I wish for happiness for everyone I know

Matthew's wish – for a safe world – and a peaceful life

I wish that we like Devon and keep our friends

I wish for world peace and humanity learning to love its home, Earth

I wish my best friends much good health and happiness

I wish all children could be free to enjoy the outdoors as much as they want

I wish I had a whole bowl of flowers

I wish for a long and healthy life

I wish Liverpool to win the League

I wish for continued good health to enjoy many more visits to Westonbirt

I would like to be a garden designer

Best wishes and happy birthday to Audrey Serafin

George W. Bush – Why, of why?

May our love grow with our faith and we pass over love onwards through time, never forgetting the place where we first promised this to each other

Why are trees green?

I wish everybody used wind power

I wish the person sticking this to the tree would smile right now

I wish that I could have a new phone and a digital camera for my birthday

If wishes come true, where would be the surprise in life?

I wish I was brave enough to dive in the deep end

I wish I had a puppy

I wish my sister would come home!

I wish for life, to be at peace. I wish health for everyone

I wish for a cup of tea

Rob Quinn to be dropped from the Rovers starting line-up

I wish my son would keep his bedroom tidy!!!

I wish for a horse

For world peace

I wish I could win the lottery and my mum would stop shouting at me!

I wish that Limelight is kept in situ

I wish I had become fit with a six pack

I wish that Julian would sell his business and give us moves!

I wish for no war and for all countries to be equal

I wish that autumn didn't come so soon

I dream for the good of the world to cease from doing nothing to stop the evil

I wish for a castle, a dragon, a garage and cars

Good health for my sister

I wish for happiness for the family

I wish for job and a decent man

Is there a heaven?

I wish I had decent handwriting

Health, wealth and happiness for all humanity and earth

I hope to be able to remember everyday that my life is in the hands of God, all day, every day no matter what, wherever I am!

I wish that I can get a corn snake when we move

I wish that J.G. is happy for life

If you want to live and thrive let a spider run alive

For peace, happiness, happy kids and a garden

No more war. Cancel world debt and make the world unite

I wish that we can grow old with things to look forward to and happiness

I wish I could see my Dad

I wish to be a games designer or rock star

That some time in the future there may be peace and I win the lottery

I wish that Nottingham Trent University would establish a chair for the study of Emperors with no Clothes

I wish to live in Australia

I wish they could stop whinging

I wish for happiness

Peace and harmony & goodwill in the family

I wish for a healthy family and world peace

I wish to visit this wonderful place again with Cate

Happiness for Sam & Paul

Kathy to get well again

I wish for health & happiness for all my family and a golden future for my boys

I wish I had a horse

That we always remember living things

My boss to get a promotion

I wish a long & happy life for all my family & friends and good health

I wish we could all see the beauty of nature

I wish Britain could have a competent prime minister

I wish for preservation of all trees

To live a full life without too many regrets, to live now

I wish my boobs were bigger my nose smaller, you know the rest!

Spend the billion on peace – not on war

We hope we have a good holiday as it has been an excellent start in the trees

Where are the WMD?!

I wish that Hannah's holiday will be all that she wishes for

My wish is for Peace to everyone, good health to all

I hope everyone moves happily towards things they wish for

It's time to grow old – I wish I could do it positively!!

I wish I knew the name of more trees

I wish for, love, peace & security just that's all

Make Rupert better

I wish for a moment in time

Peace in the world and ending of greed

May S find a partner & family

Happiness is the sun shining throu' the trees

I wish my hair was as long as Rapunzel

I wish I could win the lottery

Peace and freedom for the world

Resolution & HGR

I wish I was in the next Harry Potter film

I wish I had Hugh Grant's mansion and a BMW M3 and that I owned Volvo

I wish everything works out with my husband's career as he wants it

Action Man DVD

I wish that my family will stay healthy for their lives!

I wish I had more land to plant more trees on

I wish that I will become an actress when I am older

I wish for a fulfilling and rich career. Thank you …

Dear God, Heal Rupert of ME with his doctor's skill and our prayers

I wish I had all the lego in the world

Col's 5 million quid! I promise not to share it with anyone

I wish that I'll get better also I would like a country retreat

We would like to know the ages of some of the Red trees

Wish I had the energy to go round again

Tolerance, Peace & Happiness

I wish for a million Bay Blades

I ask for true friendship, a sense of belonging and clear purpose

I wish the ones I love a healthy and wealthy life xxx

I wish for my grandad to rest in peace. Harry William Tindell who died on 6.9.03 aged 86. God bless. Always in our thoughts.

I wish for peace in the world

I wish I can be a skyscraper architect & design roller coasters when I'm older

I want peace in the world – win the lottery – Jane finds peace; to see as many countries as possible before I become unable

I want to have as much time with Sherri & Caroline

It's my birthday and I wish for peace all over the world

I wish I could play football for England

I wish I had a Robot 'friend'

I wish there was a model shop in our village

I wish for calm and happiness in the future

Please may we be blessed with a healthy child

I wish for a pond

I wish I would become a chef

A healthy and happy family for Katie & I

I wish for incredible healthy & happiness

I wish for water

Why does Isabel love bamboo?

I wish I could jump inside the TV

I wish the … could all be very happy

I wish there was world peace

England not in Europe

I wish for health & happiness

I wish …

We wish for a child … somehow

I wish for PEACE & an end to warfare

I wish you had some litter bins

World peace and food for all

I wish for health and happiness for those I love

The gospel to all the world & Second coming

I wish 4 my dream home to be soon

I wish that everyone could be happy & have chances to create

World full of childrens' pasta

I wish for everyone to believe in God

How many trees are there?

I wish I go everythink that woude mak me one of the bested people

I wish that I make the right decision

A wish for all my 5 grandchildren

Wish my garden was tidy

I wish man would learn to live with nature and sustain the environment

When did you plant the trees?

I wish for sanity to prevail & peace in Iraq

I wish for my children to keep their rooms tidy

I wish that there be other life in the universe when I am alive. Thank you!

I wish Brittany loved me

I wish for places like this to always be here

Let's hope that MA goes OK

I wish that I had a dog

I wish that Peter and Laurie would moan less and behave better

I wish Andy and I are always happy and see the pleasure in each new day together

I wish this tree would last for ever

I wish that I will never have to be involved in a conflict

My wish is for mankind to consider that he is part of nature

Please make Papa Augusta better & all my ill friends – Sue, Phil & please deliver the Mconity grandchild safely

The world to live I harmony with nature

Good Health

I wish I had more wishes

I wish Gabi was well again

I wish for Charlotte, William & Robyn love, laughter & happiness in all their days

Reflections from the trees give out beauty which surrounds us

I wish for happiness in life

I wish for peace in the Middle East – we'll need all the prayers we can get

I wish Claire could see this tree; she probably can! xx

I wish that mankind learns to respect and conserve the environment

I pray for peace in my life and untold happiness Amen

I wish I could turn back time to perfect the mistakes I really regret

Thank goodness for some peace

I love daddy

I wish that the Purdoms & Couves meet up again soon for another picnic

I wish to be a pirate

I wish for peace in Israel/Palestine

I wish that Cliff & I will have some more years together as we are getting pretty old. Thankyou tree xx

I wish to climb trees faster

I wish for Ice Cream & Chocolate

I wish for a successful design partnership

Health and happiness to my family and friends

I wish I could marry Rick Plant

In the future will there be rockets that hover?

All our familys safe in Australia & NZ

I wish we could win the lottery PLEASE

I wish I have a happy and healthy family

I hope I have lots of fun on holiday cos I'm on holiday

I wish I was in the next Harry Potter film

I wish Calum and Ruby happiness forever

Why do people say money doesn't grow on trees when paper comes from trees?

I wish I could be a gardener like Alan Tichmarsh

I wish for Cambridge to acknowledge my brilliance and give me a place! And I wish for £3000 to work with … in Thailand

I wish to win the lotto – Please

We wish our children would find the paths for life & partners for life

I wish I'm a millionaire

I wish for a successful, enterprising, creative, wonderful life for myself

I wish that everybody knew that everyday is equal & everyone was treated equally!!

Will I angle in my rest?

I wish for love and peace to enter my life again

What else will the Kelly enquiry reveal?

I wish to be an idiot with someone working for me

My wish is to win the lottery

I wish I had a puppy

I wish for a TV and a snake

I wish Jon would make up his mind

Maak de papa van Stefan, HANS Lelemad beter!

Love is the greatest thing – love shared by humans for each other, love of the beauty around you love of God's whole creation

I wish the sycamore setting to remain as it is now

Peace and FREEDOM in the family and in the world

Ham, Egg & chips & a pint of beer on a sunny day

Plant many trees

I wish Stephen my grandson Bon Voyage

I wish that our son William grows up happy and healthy

That everyone got 'IT'

More Sea

I wish I marry Brittany Orthan in my class 7 lower at the Beacon

Lots of Land

I wish the tomatoes were here

I wish I wasn't so damned good looking

I wish for a happy fulfilling life

I wish to feel well again

I wish for the eternal peace of trees

Good health to all of us

I wish I could be top of my class!

I wish you well

I wish for a digger

Give me patience!

A wish for the family to be 100% well again and that happiness will return to us all

I wish for a tractor & a train when I am in Canada

I wish for a continuing happy relationships with my family

I wish I had a waterfall in my garden

Best wishes and long life to the new baby Serafin

I would like and wish for John (my partner) to have a long & healthy life. Thank you

I wish I had everything I want

I wish that someday me and my school could sing again in the Albert Hall

I wish to win Lottery so I can help sum people

I wish I could be an actress

I wish everyone's dreams come true

How lucky to have the company of friends

Unit will be happy and full of love

For Elvis & Agnes to be

I wish that when I am older & I will own a Farmhouse & Dog Kennels

I wish global warming would stop, the world would then not fall apart

I wish love to be made law

To regain what is lost

I wish for long life & happiness

I wish I was a pro surfer such as Sunny Garcin

Freedom & Justice for all

I think I need to become more organised with my time

I wish I was a Millionaire

To have a happy & good life with mummy & daddy

I wish for an Autumn as beautiful as the summer

Who is Number 0?

I wish for a Cat

I wish I will play for Stoke when I am older

I wish I had more time to relax

I wish for all the trees to grow old & die happy

I wish for peace in the world

I wish I could have a secret den

I wish for everybody in my family to be safe

I wish for Happiness & Creativity

I wish for Love & Peace in the world

I wish for long & happy lives for my Family & Friends

I wish for Hope & Happiness

I wish everyone to live in Peace & Tranquillity

Lucy likes the red bench too

I wish to have five children

I wish for a Healthy & Happy Life

I wish I was in the Dragons

I wish that English oak trees survive

To have my lichen (?) house in crorser

Call this art? Torturer!

I wish to be thin, female and immune to be cancer

Real princesses all of them

When I see a horse I feel can't get beat at the racecourse let me have the courage to put lots of money on it

I wish that my rabbits live a happy healthy life and that they could learn Japanese

To reach total contentedness

I wish my mom was ded

I wish I had Shiy shod

Ship from Harry I am

I wish I could be a marmot

I wish pepol would live happy

I wish I will play 15 2pac alive or with biggy in the sky for st

I've never seen so much twaddle in my life!

For Hana for Cindylou for Andrew for Charlotte for Eric and Liayse for me love

I wish for a dog

I wish for Pokemon Ruby

To find a place to live

I wish to go to seaside

Why is Tony Blair such a wanker?

I wish that Tome Colemon fancied me & he would respect me & I wouldn't feel stupid I'd no wat 2 talk about also I want to be friends with Ellen, Cat, Rach & I want to be happy with 2 girls & a dog & husband when I'm older

To be phase III wish that William will grow up to be happy & Healthy

I wish to do well & earn more money!

I wish for - man in the world

I wish for a cure for cancer and autism

Rene wants Liz to be the one

I wish I could fly

When I'm sad and lonely, when all hope is gone, when I walk along High Holborn, I think of you with nothing on

I wish for no nasty surprises

I wish for a puppy (any sort of kind)

I wish for world peace and tranquillity throughout the land

I would like to be a totally spice girl

I wish to find love & happiness with James P xxx

I wish for everyone to enjoy life

We wish for Pure to get better

Do you feel happy with yourself?

I want to be happy (& rich!)

I wish for faith

I wish for Melanie not to be afraid

I wish Darren & I stay happy together for the rest of our lives & to have wonderful children in a happy home

I wish I lived by the sea. Me too!

An end to man's inhumanity to man!

Ich Wünsche mir eine liebe frau

My earlier wish was granted. Fay sold her house in Swindon. Thank God for His goodness

Please could you make Pat, Pay & Lyon come to Mexico

A good holiday with Rosa

I wish for the problems surrounding me to be sorted out

Heath and Happiness for all the family

Why was I born?

I wish Tracey, Gary, Coral, Grace Mick & me good health

Health & happiness before wealth

I wish all wars would cease

I wish to be always as happy as now. The present

I wish for the world's people to all love one another

I wish that the world was as peaceful as Westonbirt

An end to terrorism & that all nations can live in peace together

I wish for this Arboretum – that it will be here forever

Peace, health, happiness and a little wealth

I want to be rich

I would like to move to a bungalow

Why is there so much hate in the world?

I wish for happiness for J

Why does my ex-wife want to take all my money?

I wish that when my new grandchild is born all will go well

I wish for inner peace within myself & the sun to shine upon the world

Health & Happiness for Duncan & I please

I wish for our son peace, love & joy

To love – not hate. To enjoy nature as it is. For all ills & problems to be resolved

Why are people so stupid?

I wish my grandchildren to have happy and successful lives

Why do people act the way they act? Is it a choice?

I wish my children are happy!

I wish good health to all of us

I wish that Liam will be with me forever

I wish 4 my life to be enriched with love with Cy. I love you x

To get well

I wish that everyone's wishes come true

Mother – we celebrate life in trees – huge ones!!

I wish for the land to be safe & to know its abundance

I wish for a safe journey

To be able to explore and admire nature

My hopes for a happy, fulfilling life for three daughters

I wish total happiness for N & S – health & wealth too x

Peace to the world

I wish my house will sell soon

Peace, love & Happiness to us & all who are heavy laden

Let Rob & I find romantic life w/each other for the rest
of our lives

I want to live to be old

I wish for no more wars and health & happiness to
everyone

I hope the world stays nice

Long loving life --------------------------!

Ich wünsche mir das unsere Liebe für alle heilsam wird

A happy and successful school year 4 Richard & Benjamin

I wish for wisdom, love & laughter for everyone

To keep the world clean

I wish for a world at peace

Deseo Salud y felicidad para mi familia y gracia paz
para todos

I wish for much happiness for many through love

Boyfriends

I wish all my family a happy life

Alexander wishes for another sandwich

I wish for trees to be admired for their beauty

Better health for Dorothea

I wish for all my children to be happy, healthy & loved

May the Earth's lungs breathe for ever

Please could you seal the hole in the ozone

I wish we both come to The 2043 Garden Festival & all
the ones inbetween

I wish for our grandson to pass all exams & get a part
time job

I wish for Delia Cullen to die peacefully and without pain

I wish to see my grandchildren grow up and be healthy
and happy

Greg's success in his 'new' business venture. Good Luck

I wish for my children to love and be loved

I wish that the family tree of Harry Lucas lives on forever

I wish for lots of beetroot

Please stay S R & T

I wish for more success with medical research

I wish for world peace - & Tolerance

I wish for Mr. H. to have good health

I wish for a planet where there is no war, no famine & no disease and where mankind can live in harmony with nature

Peace the world over

Ich wünsche mir, das Manfred zu mir zurück kommt

Good Health for all the family

We wish that Manchester City win a cup!! 27 years … The Premiership within 3 years would be nice

Wishing safe travels on the roads as well as life

More love, more trees

I wish for Simon to be relaxed with the children

One sky, one world – second Sunday in October each year – I wish all the world would join in & fly kites for peace

Why are we never satisfied?

I wish Alun would show he loves me

I wish for love and happiness and for Mr. Bleach!!

To be filled with love

I wish for love & peace & another child if God wills

A long and a healthy life

I wish that 'powerful' people would realise that it carries responsibility to others

I wish for world peace & the happiness of all humanity

Why does it take two to Tango?

I wish to win the lottery

I wish to have peace of mind, wherever I am & in whatever I do

Will my wife open up to me?

£10 million on the Lottery before end of 2003

Peace in this world and peace in myself

I wish for people to be kind to animals

I wish for good health and for true love …

I wish for more tranquillity and inner peace

I wish that everyone will find contentment within themselves

I wish the solicitor would phone & set a date soon! Thank you, come again

I wish I could remember the Latin names for some shrubs

I wish for better public transport to Westonbirt

I wish for our Spanish adventure to be full of health, happiness & good fortune

Hope David's marriage will be saved or meet somebody nice & me too

I wish for Gabriel x

I wish 4 luv, peace, & happiness, joy, warmth and luck, health and sanity & all these things 4 my friends

May the world know peace again. Calm & love

I hope that people like this place

To all departed friends – FLY HIGH – where the winds are free

Good luck & good health to all

I wish that we shall all fulfil our potential

I wish for my Mum – Irene – to be safe & well

I wish that the move to Spain will go well & and we will all live out our dreams

I wish I could stop swimming through treacle

I wish that I may bring happiness to those around me

True happiness throughout

I wish for peace in the world & and in our families & friends

I wish for a healthy child

To live so long that the County Treasurer sends a gunman out to shoot me

Fresh air, lush green grass, rainbow flowers, fragrant plants, sunshine, smiles & summer rain

I wish for true happiness throughout my life

I wish for my 2 girls to get ready for school on time with no arguments

Joy & laughter for the rest of my life

What is 'NORMAL'?

Beware the one way

Peace to the world

I wish that Bignet will have sex with me again

I wish for inner peace & lots of money

Health, happiness & love

Health & Happiness from us to all

I wish that my husband & I have good health & happiness

I wish Sara good year 4

For Alex & Jenny to have a long & happy marriage

I wish for a lively quiet home!

What shall I do about the two men that I love? X

I wish for more time –

All my family a good & happy life

Wats it all about

For a happy & fulfilled life

I wish I had more space to write a wish

Boyfriends

What are all the trees called?

Wish for happiness

Jemima, Tony's Haven x

Why

I wish that me n Hazel have a incredible life together and that all our dreams come true. Also that humans sort themselves out!

I wish to stay well and live to be an old lady

I wish to get a degree

A wish for health and happiness

Our wish for others to enjoy Westonbirt for many years to come

I wish an end to Iraq war. Love U trees

I wish for Debbie to stop smoking

I wish to be on my own, with my children

How long?

I wish everybody has a happy life

True Peace and happiness for all who visit this beautiful place

I want my boys to be happy

Bit more info on labels? Common names, Habit, Growing conditions, Soil, Ultimate size etc

I wish that all children could enjoy their childhood before premature adulthood

When will love be the most important thing?

I wish for peace & harmony & good health for all

Life long and happiness for all my family xx

I wish everybody love & happy life

For Jae to be OK

I wish for peace for the Whole World

I wish that mum gets a little house soon

I would like a new home with a big kitchen please

Love & happiness come to me soon & for Jan, Keith &
a chance for Mr Yates soon

I wish for a long life of love & happiness with the
people I love around me

Will we go to Canada next year?

I wish my friends Linda & Joe more happiness in their
lives

I wish or a peaceful & caring world

I hope the weather is nice for Jean's birthday party
tomorrow

Happiness, health & love for Mathilda, Harry & Andrew
(& me too!)

A beautiful healthy baby for Caroline & Vassos

I wish for lots of love & peace to come my way

I wish I had another wish

I wish I could rediscover the Tasmanian Wolf!!!

Have you visited www.TheAntiEmilyUnit

How many stars are on the sky 25.01.2007

Inner calm, total happiness & perfect peace

Wish I'd chosen the right pair of socks!

Can I have a yellow one?

Why?

I wish I could see a distant country

I wish for a big house by the sea & we won't have to
work again!

I wish a handsome prince would come from far away
& we'll get married!

I wish for two bunnies

We wish to be in love & happy together forever

Good health to ally my plans

I wish for money to help the poor

I wish chops would have a brain transplant

Health & happiness

How many turnips have I eaten?

I wish I had a sniper rifle

What could be better than this

I wish I could have a PS2

Why are people so mean to each other?

Why does the world have to be so mean?

I wish that I could be a football star when I grow up

How are we still here?

Pab & Rosh come home soon

What happens to trees in Autumn & Winter

I wish for no more of that idiot Tony Blair!

I wish nobody would read my wish

He will see clearly – the rain has gone

Why are we?

If the answer is 23 what's the question?

Casper & David & Gareth – Happiness

May John make a full recovery

I wish that god will love me

I wish our elected & unelected leaders would take
responsibility for world peace & justice seriously

I wish to be happy & healthy

I wish for more time to spend with my family & the
ability to keep them safe, well & prosperous

Thanks for 40 happy years

I hope my post engine works properly

I wish I could stay here forever

I wish common sense was the new science/Technology

What is life without music & comedy?

I wish I was with Rapunzel

I wish that all my family & loved ones be well, happy
& rich

May a very special person find peace & enjoyment

I wish to find the perfect wave!

I wish for excellent good health for us all

What is it about men?

Be one, be well, hold tight, cast a spell

I wish of Wales

I love Ken, I love Ken

May there be peace in the world for everyone

I wish to have a happy marriage

Time eternal, time to be, time is all I wish

Wish I win a lot of money soon

I wish that Carl & I will find love, happiness and be friends

If 42 is the answer, what was the question

I wish I were creative enough to think of a question

I wish for Mummy & Daddy to always love me

Lots of happy holidays

I wish to become a professional ballerina

We wish for the cessation of suffering

I wish for snow

I wish people would slow down & look around them

That my family will always be happy

I wish that my whole family will find happiness, contentment & success soon please

Wish for more tolerance between our fellow human beings

I wish for a dancing Cinderella doll

I wish for a miracle for Robert

I wish health, love, happiness & wealth to all my family & friends

To win the Rollover on Sat 13.9.03

I wish to learn how to behave adoringly

We have been married 5 years today. We wish for lots & lots more years together

I wish to be happy & healthy & the same for my family, friends & animals

Why is snot green?

I wish to come back here with my children

I wish for a new train set for my birthday

Peace on earth & countries to get on together to save this beautiful world

People to love & respect one another

I wish I had a garden like this

I wish that mr Blobby was my friend

I wish that people would take me seriously

What I want is happiness

I want to love the world & to love my friends to the end

Peace for all who want it. Happiness no misery in
the news

I wish I could watch it snow

I wish for an irish wolfhound + a couple of goats

I wish happiness for my family and everyone else

I wish for an answer to the Canadian question

Huw wishes he could be Captain Hook in a show

Please make Laura a good girl

I wish for presents I wish I was a Ballerina I wish I was
a mermaid

I wish for tolerance the whole world through

I wish there was a horse paddock here

I wish all to be well with Cathy. I wish all to be well with
all of us

Peace to all the world, soon please

I wish Noah grew up as strong and handsome as this
tree

I would like a Barbie bike please

I wish for a little baby brother

I wish I had some make up

I wish all the people in the world would meet here on a
regular basis

I wish to have a big swimming pool

I wish my mummy to get better

I wish all the big old trees had their age on the label

I wish Audrey would come back

We wish for world peace

I wish I could have a wishing fairy

I wish that I had a pony

I wish for rain in Spain, France, Portugal, Germany and
wherever it is needed

Good health and a much bigger family

I want to grow up to be a rose fairy princess

I wish to be happy forever

I wish for a dog

I wish my husband will be happy after his operation
and will be truly happy even if we have to move to
Devon again

I wish that the world and its people would stop destroying itself/themselves

I wish for a baby sister called Emily

Please bring peace into the world

I wish for happiness for Jenny and Julian a lovely couple

I wish to find a way to harmonise my own happiness with that of others

I wish people didn't drop litter

I wish for a round the world open return ticket x3

Never look back to see what might have been

I wish for a baby sister

I wish for lots of big trees

Please let my dear wife get well

I wish for more info about ages and origins of trees here

Wish everyone we know health, wealth and happiness

We want everyone to be happy

I wish that I could fly

I wish my dad had recovered in Norway (and caught that salmon) I love you, Pa

I wish live forever

I wish I could find happiness in my work

I wish to beat cancer

I wish I could separate my head and heart

I wish I had a pony

I wish I got a real platypus and swim with it

I wish for a stronger right wrist

Thomas wishes – Alex would cuddle me – and he can see the clangers set off in the space garden

Health and happiness for my lovely family

Daddy will come to France with us

I wish that all your dreams are fulfilled

To be stress free and happy together

I wish for happy peaceful times

Repeal section 28 – equality for lesbians + gay men

I wish that Emma + Zoe have a lovely time with Grandma and Grandpa

I wish for a dog that can do my homework and to go fishing with me

I wish Elodie, Toby, Jackie + Gareth lived here in Oxfordshire instead of San Francisco

I wish to move into my new house with my wonderful family

I wish to find my place in the world

I wish for lots of water toys to have fun with I wish for global peace

Pork chop chops

I wish for happiness and financial freedom for my loved ones and I

I wish I had a puppy

My wish is all the children we know and love will have a good life

I wish that I will be a famous saxophone player and have lots of money

How old is the oldest oak tree?

I wish for family health and happiness forever

I wish I had the biggest strawberry in the world

I would like air conditioning at work

I wish that the rest of the world was as peaceful as Westonbirt

I wish to find love, I hope I fall in love

I wish to walk on beaches all my life

I wish Carla in 7b will go out with me

I wish that the faraway tree lives in our garden

Please can I have a big train set

I wish I dident have to moov house

I wish the snow will come down often

I wish my love finds a job in Barcelona so he can stay with me forever

Wish that all humanity appreciate what is right here

I wish I were a wombat

I wish I could fly

I would like another cat

I make a wish for a bigger house and garden

I wish I had a big field with a pony in it

I wish I had a little sister

I wish that I will never die

How will I experience God at my time of death?

I wish that the world is a peaceful place and I wish that their was no violence

I wish for five afters of chocolate

End of all wars peace, prosperity and happiness

I wish I could marry my baby brother & live with mummy & daddy parents

I wish Adam didn't bring his own stereo machine on all hikers trips he goes on

I wish that whatever wish I make that would always come true

I wish my mum and dad wode be nise

I wish Chitty Chitty Bang Bang was true

I wish for the people of the world to enjoy peace and no war

I wish I could have everlasting wishes that come true

Will I see my friends again?

To be more to those who mean so much to me & be able to afford to be more generous. Thank you for such a beautiful place

I wish mankind would finally understand and respect nature

I wish for a lovely wife

I wish I can swim with dolphins

I wish for inner contentment and someone special to share my happiness with

I wish I could have 2 more Beyblades

I wish I would have love

I wish I could help everyone less fortunate than I

I wish for a new job

That Christopher and I have a long and happy life together

7 trains and 7 coaches

Will I live to be 103 like a tree?

I wish for a sheep

City to win the league

Peace and love time for caring

I hope I live a long and happy life

In our lives of plenty, why do we want?

I wish I could be in S Club and be a pop star

I wish you had more ribbons

I wish I got lots of money to buy lots of things with

I wish for a pay rise for all scientists bar one

I wish I was a penguin

I wish I was a tree

I wish to have an insite into the point I have of being

I wish I had a bigger bedroom it's too small

I wish there were no more wars and people stopped hurting themselves

I wish ... please save all the world's trees for future generations

I wish to find true happiness before I die

I wish for a cricket net in the garden

I wish I met the actor of Harry Potter or meet the real one and marry him. Just win the lottery every week

I wish that we win our case and get 60 thousand pounds back soon

I wish the tree that this is on could tell us all that it has seen

I wish I was a chicken

I wish I could wish

Why can't the clouds be strong so you can walk on them?

I wish mum and dad die after me

I wish I could find another job

I wish I could fly like a bird

I wish I had a tooth out

I wish that I would grow bigger (and stop having to potty train)

I wish I could see fairies

I wish I could have a dog

I wish that people were as nice as trees

I wish I could go on an aeroplane

I wish for love not war, food for the starving

I wish the holidays would go on forever

I wish I was an ultra mega dega, really really famous dude

I wish to go out with rob

I wish that I was a piece of cheese

I wish minnow our old cat will come back and live forever

I wish to get a game cube